It started with a blank wall. Interiors star Maitri Mody's first studio, with its plain white walls and prewar charm, wasn't just an apartment; it was a reset button. She asked herself, *What do I want this space to feel like?* The answer was crystal clear: joy. Bold, bright, fierce, unstoppable joy.

In *Dopamine Design*, Maitri shows you how to create a space that feels like the ultimate vibe check—effortless, playful, and 100 percent you. This book dives into all things dopamine decor—how it works, why it works, and how you can make it work for you. Inside you'll learn how colors, textures, and layouts can totally shift your mood and how to use them to create a space that feels like a hug from your favorite person. The book gets into the nitty-gritty: practical tips for working with what you've got, whether you're decorating a rental on a budget or going all out on your forever home.

Chapters include:

- Learning—adding a little playfulness and the element of surprise, because design should be fun.
- Pleasure—infusing your space with nostalgia, personal touches, and feel-good details.
- Mood—using color schemes to set the vibe in any room.
- Movement—creating flow with textures, lighting, and layouts that just work.
- Motivation—designing spaces that hype you up and make you want to be your best self.

Dopamine Design inspires you to embrace the colorful, daring, and lively to create a space—and a life—filled with things that bring whimsy and delight. Studded with 100 smile-inducing photographs, eight home tours from popular designers, actionable step-by-step tips, and renter-friendly advice, *Dopamine Design* is the only guide you'll ever need for crafting your own unique happy place.

DOPAMINE DESIGN

Meet Ari—my ultimate source of joy. This custom pug-inspired coffee table in his likeness sparks a smile every time I walk by.

MAITRI MODY

DOPAMINE DESIGN

Creating a Home That Makes You Happy

TEN SPEED PRESS
California | New York

CONTENTS

Averie Cole's Jersey City apartment perfectly captures the spirit of dopamine decor—bold, joyful, and bursting with charm.

This IKEA Pax wardrobe and DIY pink-painted dresser are the definition of functional fun. Bonus: The open closet holds outfits for both Ari and me.

INTRODUCTION

The Pink Wall

The first swipe of pink felt like freedom. It wasn't just about covering a white wall—it was about reclaiming my space, my choices, my *life*. A few months earlier, my ten-year marriage had ended, leaving me with a bruised heart, a tiny studio on the Upper West Side of New York City, and a desperate need for a fresh start.

That studio, with its plain white walls and prewar charm, wasn't just an apartment; it was a reset button. A blank canvas, where I made the rules. Actually, scratch that—there were no rules. Only possibilities.

Rolling pastel pink paint across the wall felt like dropping the mic on my old life. It was like my soul let out a happy little squeal. For the first time, I was making a space that felt like *me*. Not "Pinterest-perfect" me or "approved by committee" me—just *me*.

Until that moment, every home I'd lived in had been compromised, inherited, never truly mine. Growing up in Mumbai, I lived with my parents and younger brother in a two-room apartment. (And when I say two rooms, I mean two rooms. Not two bedrooms. Just two hardworking spaces pulling triple duty.) Our living room wore a lot of hats: homework station, dining room, guest lounge, and, by night, shared sleeping space. Everything in our home was practical—the furniture, the decor, all of it.

But creativity found its way in through other outlets: I sketched glamorous outfits, mixed bold colors and patterns in my clothes, and jumped at every art class my mom could find. I learned early on that creating something with your own hands brings a kind of magic that can't be explained—only felt.

Years later, that ingenuity sparked in my childhood became my career. I studied fashion in Mumbai, styled for music videos and commercials, and worked on editorial shoots. My days were a kaleidoscope of colors, textures, and ideas, and I thrived on the fast pace and creativity of it all.

But when I got married and moved to the United States—Jersey City, New Jersey, to be exact—everything shifted. My dependent spouse visa meant I couldn't work, and without the career I'd built to anchor me, I felt unmoored. So, I decided to go back to school, this time at the Fashion Institute of Technology in New York.

Those two years of school changed everything. I earned a bachelor's degree in International Trade and Marketing for the Fashion Industries, graduated summa cum laude, and even received scholarships from Ralph Lauren and Cotton Incorporated. Walking across the stage at graduation was one of my proudest moments. It wasn't just about the accolades—it was about proving to myself that I could start over and carve a new path, no matter what life threw at me.

But it wasn't until my then-husband's job took us to London that I really found my calling. London is like a design love letter in 3D—pastel townhouses in Chelsea and Notting Hill, mint-green Figaros casually parked on cobblestoned streets, and doors painted in colors so bold they practically dare you not to smile.

Believe it or not, I wasn't always a pastel person—far from it. Before London, pink wasn't even on my radar. Now? I'm 100 percent team blush. One walk through a candy-colored street in May, and I was done for. The way those dreamy pastels popped against the gray sky? Instant love affair.

Evening walks became my thing. I'd peek through those enormous windows (respectfully!) and catch glimpses of gorgeous, jewel-toned interiors so perfectly styled they felt like still-life paintings.

A DIY dresser in lilac with checkered knobs turns this corner into a dreamy vanity. Lilac and peach? A color match made in decor heaven.

And don't even get me started on the flowers. Rose arches. Wisteria-covered townhouses. Cherry blossoms fluffier than cotton candy. I used to not be able to tell the difference between a peony and a petunia. Now I'm a flower girlie for life. I learned to pause and take in the beauty of small moments. Flowers became my daily reminder that even the simplest details can transform how a space feels.

It was during those London years that I launched an Instagram account with my beloved pug, Ari, called @honeyidressedthepug. It started as a fun side project—dressing us in matching outfits, experimenting with pattern and color, and fully embracing the playful side of fashion. Ari was the star, and I was his loyal stylist. But what began as a creative outlet soon turned into something bigger, planting the seeds of what would eventually become a career in content creation.

Fast-forward a few years to another big move, this time back to New York. After a long stretch of trying to make it work, I ended my marriage, and I found myself starting over in that small studio apartment on the Upper West Side. Standing there with an open can of pink paint and a roller in hand, I let it sink in.

There was no one else's opinion to consider. It was just me (and Ari, of course). I asked myself: *What do I want this space to feel like?* The answer was crystal clear: joy. Bold, bright, fierce, unstoppable joy. The kind that dances on tables and wears sequins to breakfast.

The pink wall was just the start. It was my rebellion against the muted, minimalist design trends that felt more like showroom inspo than real life. Next came flowers, fairy lights, and a purple-checkered wall—because why should your home whisper when it can sing? Layer by layer, I added touches that made the studio feel uniquely mine—pops of color, whimsical patterns, and exuberant flourishes. Piece by piece, I turned it into a home that wasn't just a place to live but also an extension of *me*.

And here's the best part: It didn't just look good—it made me *feel* good. Coming home wasn't just a routine; it was a reset. No matter how messy or exhausting the world outside felt, my apartment was my sanctuary. It was a reminder that home is where your happiness begins. Somewhere between the pink wall and the fairy lights, I discovered a kind of magic I now call dopamine decor.

The devil's in the details, and this vanity is all about thoughtful finishing touches that make the space sing.

JOSH

Michael Pybus's bedroom proves that saturated colors can be beautifully balanced. The design is anchored by a wooden nightstand and spotlighted by a vintage Ettore Sottsass Tahiti lamp.

A Style That Feels Like Home

You don't have to go through heartbreak to understand the power of a home that fills you up. Maybe you've felt it walking into a friend's house that smells like strawberries and cream and feels cozy in all the right ways. Or maybe it's that one corner of your home—a favorite chair in the sunlight, a shelf stacked with your go-to books, or a rainbow rug soft beneath your feet—that makes everything feel right.

It's not about having the perfect space. It's about making your space feel perfect for *you*.

For years, design trends worshiped minimalism. White walls, neutral furniture, and barely-there decor dominated Instagram feeds and Pinterest boards. But let's be honest—minimalism isn't for everyone. It's a look, not a feeling. Dopamine design flips the script. It's not about following rules or trends. It's about creating a home that celebrates your quirks, your story, and your joy.

It's messy. It's bold. And yes, it's totally personal.

The Science of Joyful Spaces

Dopamine is basically your brain's hype man. It's the thing that gives you a little burst of happiness when you eat something amazing, hear your favorite song, or finally crush a goal. It's your brain's way of saying, *Hey, you're doing great—keep it up!*

But what does dopamine have to do with your home? Honestly, everything. The colors, textures, and even the random little objects in your space can totally influence your mood, whether you realize it or not. Think about it: A dimly lit restaurant gives you completely different vibes than a sun-drenched kitchen. Colors work the same way—vivid yellows can give you energy, while soft blues make you want to chill. Your environment has *power*. It can either pump you up or totally drain you.

Dopamine design is about taking control of that energy. It's about filling your space with things that inspire joy and make you feel good every single day.

When I painted my first pink wall, I didn't know any of this. I wasn't thinking about brain chemicals or design theory. I just wanted a space that made me happy. Looking back now, I get it: That pink wasn't just a color—it was a permission slip. It was me saying, *This is my space, and I get to decide how it feels.*

This vibrant corner in Marianne Plaisance's home features offbeat elements, like a faux cake and oversized paintbrush. It's a bold example of boundary-pushing decor that still feels cohesive.

TELL THE TRUTH
AND RUN

From Pink Walls to a Movement

What began as a personal project to heal and start fresh ended up resonating with so many others. I didn't think that my followers who were mostly there to see matching outfits with Ari would enjoy home content as much. But the questions kept pouring in: How do you choose colors that work together? Where did you get that chair? How can I make my rental look like this without losing my deposit?

That's when it hit me—I wasn't alone. There were so many people looking for ways to ditch boring, beige-on-beige spaces and create homes that actually felt *alive*. Especially during the pandemic, when our homes became our everything: office, gym, social hub. Suddenly, those minimalist spaces that looked great in magazines weren't cutting it anymore.

We wanted color. We wanted pattern. We wanted *fun*.

This book is my way of answering all those questions and sharing what I've learned along the way.

An Invitation to Joy

Let's get one thing straight: Dopamine decor isn't about following rules or copying what someone else is doing on Instagram. It's also not about overconsumption. It's about figuring out what *actually* makes you happy and bringing that vibe into your home. For me, it's bold colors, playful patterns, and a little bit of whimsy. For you? Who knows! Maybe it's all about cozy neutrals with pops of neon, or maybe you're into maximalist chaos. The goal? To help you create a space that feels like the ultimate vibe check—effortless, playful, and 100 percent you.

In this book, we're diving into all things dopamine decor—how it works, why it works, and how you can make it work for you. We'll talk about how colors, textures, and layouts can totally shift your mood and how to use them to create a space that feels like a hug from your favorite person. We'll also get into the nitty-gritty: practical tips for working with what you've got, whether you're decorating a rental on a budget or going all out on your forever home.

Each chapter will break down one of the core pillars of dopamine decor:

- **Learning: Adding a little playfulness and the element of surprise—because design should be fun.**
- **Pleasure: Infusing your space with nostalgia, personal touches, and feel-good details.**
- **Mood: Using color schemes to set the vibe in any room.**
- **Movement: Creating flow with textures, lighting, and layouts.**
- **Motivation: Designing spaces that hype you up and make you want to be your best self.**

Afraid of committing to color? Start small. A painted shape around a floral shelf is a simple, joyful entry point.

You'll also find home tours, design tips, and dopamenus, which include sensory and emotional "ingredients" you can add to your space to spark delight, creativity, and motivation. Each course—Appetizers, Mains, and Desserts—represents a different intensity of experience, from subtle hits of pleasure to full-on dopamine feasts.

My dopamine decor journey started as my way of taking back my life. My studio apartment was my chance to start over. It was about turning a blank space into something colorful, messy, and perfectly imperfect—for both me and my partner in crime, Ari the pug.

Back then, it was just the two of us figuring things out, one fairy light at a time. I wanted our home to feel like a haven—cozy, inviting, and full of personality. And somewhere along the way, I realized something big: Creating a home isn't just about healing or starting over. It's about celebrating who you are right now.

Dopamine decor is about letting your space reflect *you*—your quirks, your vibe, your story. It's about finding joy in the small things, like a perfectly styled corner or a color combo that just makes you smile.

So whether you're here to add a pop of color to your beige-on-beige walls or to completely transform your space, my hope is that this book inspires you to play, experiment, and have fun. Your home isn't just where you live—it's where your life happens. So why not make it a place you *love*?

The lilac accent wall in this dining nook is made all the more impactful by a matching locker. The cheetah lamp and Frida Kahlo painting by Olaf Hajek add flair.

BUTTER

CHAPTER ONE

LEARNING

Making, Mending & Finding Your Flow

Ghislaine Viñas's expertly curated coffee table showcases an ever-evolving mix of favorite books and quirky collected objects.

There's a real magic in making something yourself—something that didn't exist before you rolled up your sleeves. It's not just about the final product (though getting compliments on your handmade lamp *is* a top-tier flex).

It's the in-between stuff that hooks you. The moment when you finally figure out how to line up your wallpaper. When your painted wall dries and looks exactly like the vision in your head (or even better!). When a pile of materials slowly starts looking like . . . something. That feeling? It's part pride, part peace, part "Wait, did I just tap into a new version of myself?"

For me, DIY became a kind of therapy. After my marriage ended and I began building a new chapter from the ground up, creating with my hands reminded me that I was capable. That I could do hard things. That I could make beauty out of the mess. Every wall I painted, every shelf I installed, every weird little decorative object I hot-glued together became a little love note to myself. I could start again, and I didn't need to wait on anyone else to make my space (or my life) feel like home.

This is what I love about DIY: it's so much more than making something—it's a kind of meditation. When you're immersed in a project, your brain quiets down. You're not spiraling about texts you shouldn't have sent or the chaos that is your inbox. You're just . . . in it. Creating. Problem-solving. Breathing.

And the hits keep coming. There's a dopamine boost when you're in flow. Another when you use the thing you made. And a bonus hit when someone says, "Wait, *you* made that?" Why, yes. I did. And it feels just as good every time.

Fear, Thread, and a Sewing Machine

I'll never forget my first DIY experience. Picture this: fashion school, patternmaking class, me staring at a sewing machine like it had personally insulted me.

I had never sewn a thing in my life. I was lagging behind, stressed, and considering faking a wrist injury just to get out of class (kidding . . . kind of). I muddled through, but over summer break, I bought a sewing machine and decided to give myself a crash course at home.

And you know what? Practice didn't make perfect, but it did make me better. I stopped dreading the machine and started falling in love with the process. There were so many little aha moments—like finally nailing a clean hem or learning how to sew a French seam that didn't unravel in the wash. These tiny wins felt huge.

Eventually, I was walking down the street wearing trousers I had made myself. Someone complimented them and I got to say, "Thanks. I made them." The serotonin hit? Unreal. It felt like I had this secret superpower—and I couldn't wait for someone else to remark on my homemade outfit.

By the time I graduated, I was making blazers with couture finishes. Sewing went from intimidating to therapeutic. And that's the kind of shift DIY can bring—it takes fear and turns it into pride.

One painted switch later and Jassy turns a standard light fixture into functional art.

Getting My Paint On

Remember that pink wall from my first apartment? Painting it was empowering. But let's be real: The process was not all pretty. As much as I wish it had played out like a dreamy montage set to a Phoebe Bridgers track, in reality, it was more like a comedy of errors involving multiple trips to the hardware store in a single day. At one point, a very tired employee gently suggested, "Maybe just . . . watch a YouTube tutorial?"

Rude, but fair.

The whole process felt overwhelming. Just figuring out what supplies I needed made me want to lie down. But I stuck with it. And now, four apartments and many walls later, painting is one of my favorite parts of decorating.

So if you've never painted before—don't worry. I did the hard stuff so you don't have to. Learn from my chaos

And speaking of painting, let me tell you about my roller hill—the one I'm willing to die on. Every time I post a painting video, someone in the comments points out, "You *know* you can use a roller with a long handle, right?" Yes. I know. I'm very aware. But long handles make my arms ache, and honestly, they're just not for me. I prefer using a short-handled roller and climbing up on a sturdy ladder. Is it the "right" way? Maybe not. But it's *my* way—and it works. The paint still gets on the wall, and I get to enjoy the result without needing a shoulder massage afterward. The DIY police haven't shown up yet, so I think I'm good.

That's the thing: Figure out what works for you. There's no one right way—there's just your way.

And once you paint one wall? There's no turning back. The process becomes joyful. The results are addictive. The before-and-after glow-up? Chef's kiss. And the best part is it's just paint. If you hate it, you can always paint it back.

Color blocking and art team up to stylishly hide an electrical box in my apartment's entryway.

Wall Paint Starter Kit

(aka how to skip the awkward chat with the hardware store guy)

PAINT TRAY
A must-have for evenly loading your roller.

DROP CLOTH
Keep your floors paint-free.

CAN OPENER AND STIR STICK
Use the little metal opener some paint stores give you or a screwdriver to pop the can, then stir the paint with a wooden stirrer.

ROLLER AND HANDLE
Choose the roller based on your wall finish—smooth or textured—plus a sturdy handle for easy application.

PAINTER'S TAPE
Go for Frog Tape for the sharpest, cleanest lines—especially if you're tackling stripes or checks.

DETAIL BRUSH
Perfect for edges and those hard-to-reach spots.

PLASTIC BAG
Wrap your roller between coats to keep it from drying out—no crusty surprises next round!

Peel, Stick, Cry . . . Repeat

True story: My first time using peel-and-stick wallpaper nearly ended with me in tears. The panels stuck together, the pattern refused to line up, and I was one misaligned seam away from tossing the whole roll out the window. But I stuck with it (pun fully intended), and eventually it got easier. Now I sometimes joke that I could apply peel-and-stick wallpaper in my sleep. Growth!

But let's be real—some DIYs just don't work out. Remember that time during the pandemic when everyone was making tile tables on TikTok? Well, I decided I had to give it a try. I had never tiled anything before, so I should have started small with a little cube side table, but instead, I ambitiously went for a full-size desk.

At the time, I was living in my first small studio apartment. Pretty much my entire apartment became my workspace for two days. I slept with grout under my fingernails. And though the desk did look cute in the end, it fully came apart not long after I put the finishing touches on it. A major DIY fail! Would I try it again? Probably not—mostly because I didn't enjoy the process of tiling. But I love watching other people do it, and I'm so impressed when it turns out beautifully.

That's the thing with DIY—it might look easy on social media, but sometimes the reality doesn't match the vision. And that's okay. It's all part of figuring out what you genuinely enjoy doing yourself and what's better left to the experts—or at least to your TikTok feed. Sometimes, it's about figuring out what's actually fun for you, and that might mean cheering on someone else's DIY from the sidelines.

Ultimately, I don't believe in "practice makes perfect." Because what even *is* perfect? Perfection's a moving target—and a boring one at that. I believe in getting better. In learning as you go. In the quiet confidence that builds every time you try something new.

Take my butter-yellow IKEA shelves. I painted them myself, and they turned out so pretty. Hanging them up, though? That was a different story. I was super precise—paper cutouts, careful markings, the whole nine yards. But when the moment of truth came, the shelves ended up about a half inch off. Not aligned. Not level. Not "perfect."

Since I live in a rental, I didn't want to drill more holes, so I left them.

And you know what? I love them that way.

When I shared the project on social media, most people felt the same way I do—and some even said, "Yep, those shelves are notoriously tricky." That made me feel a little less alone in the wonkiness.

I gave this rental kitchen a glow-up with contact paper cabinets and peel-and-stick wallpaper on the fridge and wall.

SMEG
DUNKIN'

But there were a few folks who could not handle the half-inch gap. And here's what I say to that: Let them be bothered.

Because the truth is, DIY is not about flawless results. It's about self-expression. About learning. About doing something cool with your own two hands and seeing what happens. And if a project starts turning into a stress spiral instead of a joyful experience? You have every right to decide that particular craft just isn't your thing. Walking away isn't a failure—it's a boundary.

You don't have to finish everything. You don't have to impress anyone. You just have to find the projects that bring you joy—and keep doing those.

Remember: Joy, not perfection, is the goal.

These days, I pick my DIYs with care. I ask myself: *Will this make me happy? Am I excited about the process, not just the product?* If the answer's yes, I'm in. If not, I'm watching someone else do it on Instagram from the comfort of my couch.

Cloud wallpaper and a curvy bed frame bring the outdoors in. A Verner Panton lamp adds just the right amount of pop.

THE LET THEM THEORY
Mel Robbins
No Worries

LG
NEW YORK CITY
FEED ME
LONDON
Subway

The Weird Stuff in My Head That Had to Be Made

Some ideas are just too specific, too strange, or too *you* to exist out in the wild. They live in your head like little gremlins, demanding to be brought to life. That's how some of my favorite DIYs were born—not from Pinterest or trends, but from sheer creative impulse.

Take my disco pendant lights. I love sparkle. I love vintage. I love iconic design. So naturally, I became obsessed with Verner Panton's Flowerpot pendants—but I also wanted them to reflect light in my sun-drenched, floor-to-ceiling-windowed living room. And while I adore those lamps, I would never dare cover an original in mirror tiles. That would be—let's be honest—design sacrilege. So I found some dupes and gave them the disco ball treatment instead. It was tedious, oddly satisfying, and completely worth it. Now every time golden hour hits and those lights start casting sparkles across the room, I feel that little jolt of "Wow, I made that."

Same with the chair I built in a woodworking class in Brooklyn. I didn't grow up around power tools. I was nervous about measuring angles, cutting wood, all of it. But the moment I nailed two pieces together and they started to resemble an actual chair? I was hooked. I even added pops of color to make it feel more me. That chair now sits proudly in one of my favorite corners of my home—sturdy, stylish, and full of heart.

DIY lets you take the weird, wonderful ideas that live in your head—the ones that don't quite exist yet—and turn them into reality. It's creative problem-solving with a personal twist. It's about asking yourself: *What would make me smile? What haven't I seen before? What could I make instead of buy?*

Not every idea turns out the way you pictured it. Some take a few tries. Some evolve into something totally different. But that unpredictability? That's part of the thrill. You're not just following instructions—you're inventing as you go.

Whether it's disco-tiled lighting or a funky chair you built from scratch, the things you make yourself carry a kind of magic. They're not just functional or aesthetic—they're physical manifestations of your creativity, your curiosity, your courage to try.

So if you ever find yourself thinking, *This is so specific and niche, no one else would ever want this*—perfect. That means it's yours. That means it's time to make it.

DIY lets you express your style, your story, your weird little obsessions. It's like fashion for your space. And the only limit? Your imagination (and maybe your lease agreement).

Mirror stickers give this Verner Panton pendant lamp dupe an instant disco makeover. A Gustaf Westman vase and pug art complete the look.

A painted checkered arch as a headboard? Yes, please. Scalloped green wall trim and pink accents throughout keep the bedroom fresh and full of spirit.

Next-Level, No Pressure

Now that I finally have a home of my own in Portland, Maine, it feels like a whole new creative playground has opened up. For so long, being in a rental meant every design decision had to be temporary—reversible, removable, undoable. But now? I have so many DIY ideas I want to bring to life that were never before possible.

It's a long and ever-changing list: pottery, floral arrangements, baking, building more furniture, and maybe even reupholstering a chair one day if I'm feeling bold. But I'm not trying to rush through it like it's some kind of checklist. I'm going at my own pace, saying yes to projects that spark curiosity and joy, and giving myself permission to leave room for the unexpected. And I know that whatever I make next will bring me the same mix of peace, purpose, and low-key meditative joy I've come to crave.

Because that's the thing about DIY: it's not just about what you make—it's about who you become while making it. Every project adds a new layer of confidence, creativity, and self-trust. And as long as I keep following that feeling, I know I'll always find my next favorite thing to make . . . even if it doesn't exist yet.

DIY Moves—5 Key Takeaways

1. START SMALL, AND STAY CURIOUS.
A painted wall. A stitched hem. A little side table. Begin with baby steps and let your skills (and confidence) grow from there.

2. FIND THE JOY IN IMPERFECTION.
Slightly crooked shelves? Iconic. A wobbly stool? Character. DIY is about joy, not flawless execution.

3. KNOW WHEN TO WALK AWAY.
If a project brings more stress than smiles, it's okay to stop. Your mental health matters more than matching wallpaper seams.

4. DO IT YOUR WAY.
Forget the "rules." Use the tools and methods that work for you. DIY is personal, not a standardized test.

5. MAKE WHAT DOESN'T EXIST.
Sometimes your dream decor isn't sold in stores. That's your cue to make it. The results will be weird, wonderful, and entirely your own.

Design Your Dream DIY Day

Take five minutes to dream up your ideal DIY day. Don't overthink it—just follow the joy. Use these prompts to guide you.

WHAT WOULD YOU MAKE (OR TRY TO MAKE)?

WHAT TOOLS OR MATERIALS WOULD YOU NEED?

WHAT MUSIC WOULD BE PLAYING WHILE YOU WORK?

WHAT'S THE VIBE OF THE SPACE YOU'D BE CREATING IN?

WHOM WOULD YOU WANT TO SHOW IT OFF TO?

When it comes to DIY, there are no rules and your home is your playground. Case in point: these neon-pink shower curtains Jassy used to reinvent his dining room window.

HOME TOUR

Marianne Plaisance

Step inside Marianne Plaisance's home and you feel like you've entered a work of art, where color, creativity, and personality take center stage. A graphic designer and photographer by trade, Marianne has always had an eye for bold, dynamic visuals. That skill translates directly into her home, where she approaches each space almost like it's a 2D composition, balancing color, shape, and contrast with a designer's precision.

Marianne's living room is a masterclass in color layering. Lime, cobalt, rainbow curtains—it's vibrant and surprisingly cohesive.

A custom sign adds an extra wink to this quirky, high-impact corner of the living room.

Marianne shares her home with her boyfriend and their pup, in a space that's as unconventional as it is stunning: a converted artist's studio inside a former bank. The building still has many of its original features—vaults, moldings, even marble floors—but she has transformed it into a joyful, high-energy space that reflects her love for dopamine decor, vintage treasures, and playful design.

Her home has become the heart of her content, too. For the past five years, Marianne has been documenting her design journey on YouTube, amassing an audience of hundreds of thousands. Her fans are obsessed with her bold, unconventional aesthetic—so much so that some have even joked that her spaces look AI-generated (which she takes as the highest compliment).

Marianne's home is a perfect balance of bold, thoughtful design and pure joy. From her rainbow curtains to her vault turned closet to her giant cherries, every piece tells a story of creativity, fun, and personal expression. Her biggest takeaway? Trust your instincts, break the rules, and create a home that makes you feel something. Because when you design with joy, your space becomes more than just a place to live—it becomes a place to *thrive*.

How would you describe your design aesthetic?

Colorful but balanced. I love maximalism, but I don't like clutter. I prefer a curated approach, where every piece has impact but nothing feels excessive or overwhelming. I think that comes from my graphic design background. I see rooms as a flat composition and try to create focal points. I want each space to feel intentional, so your eye knows exactly where to go.

Which items in your home would be the most coveted in a future estate sale?

My green couch, for sure! Everyone always asks about it. But for me, the most special pieces are the two portraits my boyfriend painted for our bedroom. They have a David Hockney feel and mean so much to me because it was his first time painting.

Polished meets punchy in Marianne's bedroom. A lip-shaped sofa, standout lights, and artwork by her boyfriend tie the pink-and-red palette together.

Giant cherries and a bank vault locker inject energy and attitude into this neutral corner in Marianne's home.

How does your home reflect your happiest memories?

I'll never forget the feeling of finally getting this home after obsessing over the listing for six months . . . it felt like fate! But more than that, it's the memories of my dad. He and I worked on a lot of the design together, installing moldings, figuring out details, et cetera.

We didn't always agree on design choices, but in the end, those little debates made the process even more special. Everything we worked on together reminds me of the time we spent bringing this home to life.

What's your favorite hidden or unexpected detail in your home that guests might overlook?

Definitely the bank vault that I turned into a walk-in closet. It's the coolest feature of my home, and most people can't believe it was once used to store money.

Are there any design "rules" you love breaking?

The idea that you need to stick to a limited color palette. I love mixing colors freely. In open spaces, I might be more intentional about balance, but in smaller rooms? I go all in. I don't follow that "three-color rule." I break it all the time!

How does your home reflect your childhood influences or cultural background?

It honestly feels like a dream house my younger self would have created. People say my space looks like a set from a Disney show, and I take that as the best compliment.

What's your secret to scoring the best vintage or secondhand finds?

Check every single day. If I really want something, I refine my Facebook Marketplace algorithm and search for it constantly.

One of my best finds? A pair of giant cherries that were originally made for a mall in Quebec. A follower actually sent me the listing, and I drove three hours to get them. Sometimes the best finds happen when your community helps!

Marianne in her show-stopping living room.

Do you have a "no regrets" splurge item that instantly brings you joy?

My rainbow curtains. I have super high ceilings, and the curtains were the first thing I installed when I moved in. They completely set the mood for the space. People forget how much curtains can transform a room!

If your walls could talk, what would they say about your design journey?

"You figured it out!" My style has evolved, but I've always had a clear vision. The biggest shift is that I trust myself now—I don't worry about trends or second-guess my instincts.

A cozy, colorful nook just for Marianne's pup. Wallpaper, art, and clever design make it feel like a mini room within a room.

ASHLEY LONG

Color-drenched but never overwhelming, Marianne's living room nails the balance. Green and yellow pop, while the artwork injects visual rhythm and depth.

What brands or designers do you keep coming back to when decorating your home?

I love Scandinavian and Nordic brands—they have an amazing design sensibility. Layered makes beautiful rugs, Tekla has great home pieces, and my lip-shaped sofa is from Heller Furniture. My green couch is from Eternity Modern, which is a Canadian brand I love.

How do you balance function with fun in your decor?

If a furniture piece isn't comfortable, I won't buy it. I live and work in my home, so function is key.

For example, I added a wall in my entryway because the space was originally too open. You could see straight through to the back of the house, and it felt awkward. The wall is practical and adds structure to the layout.

I also designed a cozy little space for my dog that fits the aesthetic of my home. It's functional for him, but it still looks intentional within the space, which was important to me.

Which DIY project or personal touch in your home means the most to you?

My giant cherries! They are the most fun, unexpected thing in my space, and they make me happy every time I see them.

What are some of your happy colors or color combinations?

Yellow! It's my ultimate happy color. There's just something about yellow. It instantly makes a space feel joyful. And when combined with bold colors like cobalt blue or softer shades like pink and turquoise, it creates the perfect balance between fun and livable.

Any advice for someone wanting to incorporate dopamine decor into their space?

Start small. Paint a coffee table, get a colorful side table, or add a bold rug. If you love it, keep going! Another fun trick? Drench a room in one color. A fully pink bedroom, for example. It's bold but totally reversible if you ever change your mind. It's one of the easiest ways to make a high-impact change without committing to a whole palette.

Spotted on Facebook Marketplace: giant cherries that became a show-stopping centerpiece.

Marianne's DOPAMENU

• APPETIZERS •

Add rainbow-colored curtains.

Create focal points to make a room feel intentional.

• MAINS •

Dream big—imagine transforming an unexpected space like a bank, church, or school into your home.

Break the three-color rule and mix colors freely.

• DESSERT •

Add exaggerated and oversized decor (like giant cherries!).

HOME TOUR

Jassy

Jassy doesn't just decorate—he performs with paint, builds with personality, and designs with unapologetic flair. A drag artist and co-founder of the queer wrestling phenomenon *Choke Hole,* Jassy brings the same energy of spectacle and satire that fuels his stage life into the rooms of his home.

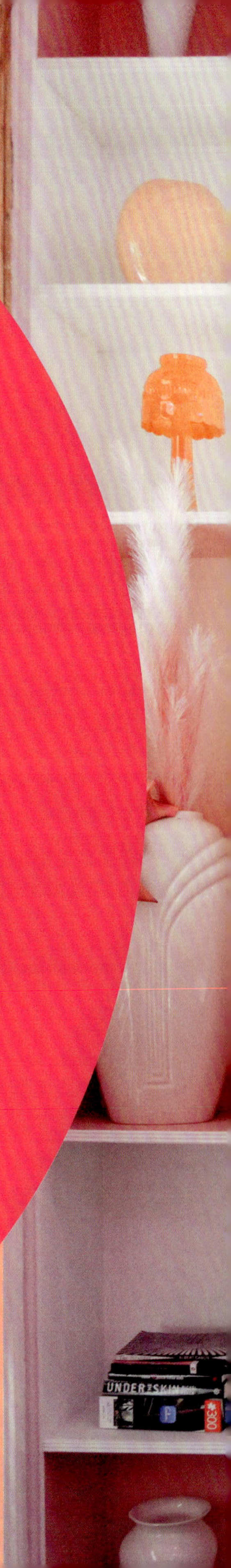

Jassy's shelf is curated and styled to perfection with a mix of books, decor, and color that draws the eye and holds it.

Raised in New Orleans, Jassy bought his home in 2020 at the height of the pandemic. With restaurants shut down and drag shows paused, he channeled all his energy into transforming his first-ever home—a classic New Orleans shotgun duplex—into a surrealist playground of color, texture, and pure visual delight. From a tiled bed to a backyard painted to resemble a pool, the house blurs the line between installation art and everyday living.

Jassy's home is a celebration of queer joy, New Orleans spirit, and fearless self-expression. It's not just a place to live; it's a portal into an alternate reality where beauty is built, not bought. Embrace color. Break the rules. Let your imagination run wild. Sometimes, your greatest design project is just waiting to be discovered—by you.

How would you describe your design aesthetic?

Surreal, vibrant, and fun! It's inspired by *Choke Hole,* the satirical drag wrestling show I produce with my closest friends. My house feels like an extension of that universe—absurd in the best way and always meant to feel joyful.

Which items in your home would be the most coveted in a future estate sale?

Definitely my vanity setup. It's a mix of hacked IKEA pieces and vintage art deco cabinets, topped with a custom orange chain mirror and an acrylic desktop. I also have a tiled bed that's totally one of a kind.

If your home had a theme song, what would it be and why?

"Groove Is in the Heart" by Deee-Lite. It's playful and funky, and it makes you want to dance. That's the vibe I try to channel with my design—something that makes you feel excited and happy the second you walk in.

How does your home reflect your happiest memories?

My friends and I have performed with *Choke Hole* in Times Square, at the Met, in Vegas, LA, Germany—even filmed a documentary. The house is a love letter to everything we've built together, and all the wild, beautiful things we've created as a collective.

It's hard to believe this one-of-a-kind vanity is a DIY. Jassy's clever IKEA hacks make it both stylish and distinctly his own.

Hand-painted abstract mural meets arched doorway—Jassy's home blends traditional bones with modern creativity.

These hand-painted arched cabinets deliver both style and storage.

What's your favorite hidden or unexpected detail in your home that guests might overlook?

My bed has a hidden outlet for charging that's disguised as tile. It blends in so well, people usually miss it!

Also, my backyard is painted to look like a swimming pool. It's ridiculous—and it makes me laugh every time I look outside.

Are there any design "rules" you love breaking?

All of them. I painted vintage art deco cabinets and a hundred-year-old brick fireplace. People get so precious about "original materials," but I think rules are made to be broken—intentionally and with style.

How does your home reflect your childhood influences or cultural background?

Growing up in New Orleans shaped everything. The city is all about celebration, authenticity, and DIY artistry—just look at Mardi Gras. My home carries that same spirit of community, weirdness, and creative freedom.

What's your secret to scoring the best vintage or secondhand finds?

Facebook Marketplace at 2 a.m. Seriously—it's when the good stuff hits.

Do you have a "no regrets" splurge item that instantly sparks joy?

Paint! I recently repainted a room with six colors and twelve gallons using an airless sprayer to create a smooth gradient effect. It was a splurge for sure, but the final look? So worth it.

If your walls could talk, what would they say about your design journey?

"You're crazy."

What brands or designers do you keep coming back to when decorating your home?

Cold Picnic, Quiet Town, and IKEA. I love a good IKEA hack. Urban Outfitters' home line is also surprisingly fun and accessible.

Jassy lounges on blue-tiled stairs that pop beautifully against deep burgundy walls.

How do you balance function with fun in your decor?

I tend to prioritize aesthetics over function. People ask how I can sleep on a tiled bed or if I stub my toe. I do. And when I cry from the pain, I remind myself they're tears of joy from the beauty.

Which DIY project or personal touch in your home means the most to you?

My tiled bed is my proudest project. My dad helped me build the base, and I did all the tiling myself—even cut my hand twice in the process! It's wild, impractical, and totally me.

No pool? No problem. Jassy painted one in his backyard, proving that sometimes joy is a brushstroke away.

Orange accents, including a DIY chandelier, create a striking contrast in Jassy's dining room.

What are some of your happy colors or color combinations?

Orange is my forever color. I wore a full neon orange outfit to Disney World when I was eight, and I've been obsessed ever since. I love pairing orange with shades of green and blue.

Any advice for someone wanting to incorporate dopamine decor into their space?

Start with DIY. When you put your own creativity into a space, you end up loving and appreciating it so much more.

Jassy's tiled bedframe, created with help from his dad, includes concealed outlets. A hot pink dresser seals the dopamine deal.

Jassy's DOPAMENU

• APPETIZERS •

Hide electrical outlets in custom furniture.

DIY a chain-link chandelier.

• MAINS •

Make your own elaborate and one-of-a-kind furniture.

Paint a swimming pool in your backyard instead of having an actual swimming pool.

• DESSERT •

Put aesthetics first—yes, even if it means function comes second.

CHAPTER TWO

PLEASURE

The Joy of Vintage & the Thrill of the Hunt

In a former tiny studio of mine, I added a little dining nook to the kitchen, bringing it to life with a lilac arch and hanging plants.

There's a reason finding the perfect vintage piece feels like hitting the jackpot—it's the thrill of the chase, the rush of the unexpected, the deep satisfaction of owning something with a story. It's a dopamine hit wrapped in a secondhand treasure. It's the kind of high you can't get from next-day shipping.

Maybe it's the wild story behind how you acquired a favorite vintage piece—like finding the perfect vase for a fresh bouquet of daisies or stumbling across an eccentric pattern that radiates joy. Maybe it's the super soft texture of a new-to-you velvet chair that instantly puts you at ease. It's the tiny, unexpected moments that make you stop, smile, and really take in your surroundings.

For me, pleasure is all about the chase (at least, when it comes to decorating!). It's about spotting that one-of-a-kind piece in a crowded flea market, the adrenaline rush of an auction countdown, or unearthing something special in the back of a dusty antique store. Unlike mass-produced decor, vintage finds have a rarity that makes them feel like a real prize. The thrill is in the search, the satisfaction in securing the item, and the joy of seeing it in your space every day.

There's also something exhilarating about the fact that money doesn't guarantee a vintage find. Sure, you might have the bank balance, but that doesn't mean the object of your dreams will suddenly appear. You have to wait for it, search for it, and hope for it. And then, when you finally stumble upon it, it's an indescribable kind of pleasure. The kind that makes you want to text your mom, shout the news from the rooftops, and maybe even shed a tear. A rush that has to be experienced to be understood.

The Science of Why Vintage Feels So Good

Let's geek out for a sec—because you know that rush when you spot a vintage piece you've been stalking like it's your long-lost soulmate, right? That's dopamine doing its thing. Your brain lights up like you just got Taylor Swift tickets at face value. Scoring a rare vintage piece gives us the ultimate high, triggering the same neural pathways that light up when you solve a puzzle or score big on a gamble. Studies show that the anticipation of a reward can actually feel even more exciting than the reward itself. That's why scrolling through listings, digging through flea market bins, or stalking an auction feels just as amazing as bringing an item home.

And then there's the element of scarcity. When something is rare—a vintage Miu Miu bag or that Luigi Massoni vanity that's been on my wish list forever—it instantly becomes more desirable. Psychologists call this the "scarcity effect." I call it "that thing where you suddenly need something you didn't even know existed five minutes ago." It's why vintage shopping feels more rewarding than buying something mass-produced—you're not just acquiring an object; you're securing something that not everyone else can have.

And on an even deeper level? Vintage shopping taps into our human need for connection. To a time, a place, a story bigger than ourselves. Every vintage piece has lived a life before it found its way to you. Maybe it sat in a 1970s lounge, or was part of someone's daily morning ritual decades ago. There's something so special about knowing that your favorite lamp, mirror, or side table was loved before you. It's basically an heirloom—just, you know, from someone else's relative.

And let's not forget nostalgia. Research shows that nostalgia boosts mood, reduces stress, and makes people feel more connected to their past. When you bring a vintage piece into your home, you're tapping into history and memory in a way that modern decor just can't replicate. Whether it's a retro Murano glass lamp or a set of hand-painted ceramics, vintage decor brings stories with it—stories that make your home feel richer, more layered, and more alive.

Some of my most precious pieces cost next to nothing. But to me, they're priceless because of the nostalgia factor. Like my vintage crystal orange juicer. When I was growing up, my mom had a plastic version of the same design, and she'd use it to make fresh juice every weekend in our Mumbai kitchen. The moment I spotted the original crystal version in a thrift shop, I had to have it. Now every time I use it, I feel a little closer to her—like she's right there with me, even though she's halfway across the world.

Another treasure of mine is my grandmother's china collection. As a kid, I never understood why she barely used it—why have something so pretty if you weren't going to enjoy it? Now I get it. It wasn't just about the beauty; it was about keeping something safe because it carried stories, history, and memories.

Then there's my grandfather's wooden cigarette holder. It's carved so that when you press a bird's tail, it lifts a cigarette in its beak. My grandfather quit smoking long before I was born, but as a kid, I'd use it to pick up pencils instead. Every time I see it in my home, I remember those little moments of fun.

The Finds That Stick with You

The vintage finds I love most aren't the ones that were easy to get—they're the ones I worked for, the ones that felt like fate when I stumbled upon them. Like my Ancona hummingbird kettle, which became an obsession. I had been coveting this vintage Italian design—complete with tulip details and a tiny hummingbird perched on the spout—for ages. When I finally found one on eBay, I entered my first-ever bidding war. The final thirty seconds? Pure chaos. Someone outbid me with five seconds left, and I had a full-on panic attack. Then, somehow, my finger managed to hit the right key at the last second and I managed to outbid them. The rush was unreal. If eBay had an MVP trophy, I'd be giving my victory speech. Honestly? I blacked out from the adrenaline and woke up holding a PayPal receipt.

In Ghislaine's home, color blocked walls and curated art make the compact powder room feel cozy and cool.

My Geoffrey Rose Frozen Moments ice cream sundae sculpture—a surrealist decor piece that looks like a towering ice cream sundae, with a stream of melted chocolate frozen in midair—is quirky and weird, and it makes me smile every time I look at it.

And my Lenox Spice Village always sparks conversation. Lenox first introduced this set in 1989 as a monthly subscription—you'd get one tiny ceramic house each month, and by the end of two years, you'd have an entire village of spice jars. Now vintage sets are selling for thousands on eBay. Lenox even reissued the set in limited quantities, and I was lucky enough to help promote the re-release. My set might be new, but it still has that nostalgic energy that makes it special.

My trusty Spice Village set by Lenox pops on a hand-painted shelf.

Lizzy's treasured vintage Alessi chrome kettle is the crown jewel of her kitchen.

The Pleasure of the Hunt

If you've ever refreshed an eBay listing over and over, hoping to get to it before someone else does, or scoured estate sales at the crack of dawn, you know that half the fun of vintage is the hunt. You never know exactly what you'll find.

There's something wildly satisfying about sifting through a pile of questionable stuff and unearthing a total gem—like finding a diamond in a dumpster. It's like treasure hunting, but instead of gold, you're walking away with a funky 1960s lamp, a designer chair from the '80s, or a mid-century walnut sideboard you never knew you needed but now can't live without.

Sometimes the best finds come when you least expect them. I once popped into a thrift store on a random afternoon walk and left with a set of vintage crystal glasses that now make every drink feel fancy. That's the magic of vintage—it's unpredictable, and that makes every win even sweeter.

But the hunt doesn't always happen in a market. One of the most thrilling ways to score vintage, especially in a city like New York? Stooping. If you're not familiar, stooping is when people leave decorative items and furniture out on the stoop or sidewalk for anyone to take. Entire Instagram accounts track stoop finds in different neighborhoods.

One of my favorite stooping stories isn't even my own—it's my friend's. She called me, breathless, and said: "I just found the perfect little dresser, but I need help carrying it." And just like that, I became a co-conspirator in a heist. We hauled it ten blocks to her apartment, dodging pedestrians and making eye contact with exactly zero cabdrivers. Now every time she looks at it, she remembers that adventure, and every time I go over, I remember it too. Vintage finds aren't just objects—they're experiences, bonding moments, memories in physical form.

Also, pro tip: If you ever find a great vintage sofa or chair on the street, don't be scared off. Just inspect seams, cushions, and crevices carefully for any unwanted hitchhikers (bedbugs are no joke!), then deep-clean it with an upholstery cleaner, and boom, it's a high-end find instead of a mystery fabric item from the sidewalk.

Sustainability: The Feel-Good Factor

It's no secret that fast furniture breaks faster than a situationship—it's all fun and games until it's not. We live in a world of overconsumption, where furniture turnover is higher than ever. Big-box retailers churn out trendy pieces that barely last a few years before ending up in a landfill.

Choosing vintage means rescuing an object, giving it new life, and keeping it out of the trash. It also means owning a quality item, often for much less than it's worth—something that was built to last, with craftsmanship that's hard to find in mass-produced decor today.

Unlike fast furniture, vintage pieces endure. The things we find today—whether it's a funky retro bar cart, a 1950s German color-blocked plant stand, or an IKEA chair from the year you were born—have already stood the test of time.

And it feels good to incorporate these items in your space. Not just because you're doing something better for the planet, but because there's a special kind of pride in knowing that you found something rare, saved it, and gave it a second life.

Making Vintage Work in Your Space

Some people worry that adding vintage will make their home feel disjointed or dated. And honestly? They're not totally wrong—if you go overboard, a space can start to feel like a museum exhibit or a *Mad Men* set instead of a real, lived-in home. The key is balance.

A space filled only with vintage can sometimes feel heavy, like it's frozen in the past. And a space filled only with modern decor can come off as a little sterile, like it's auditioning to be a dentist's office instead of a home. The sweet spot is mixing the two, and even mixing the eras. Too many pieces from one decade can start to feel like a set design instead of a lived-in space. Think of it like mixing the perfect mocktail. A little vintage, a little modern—too much of one thing and the balance is off.

Pair a 1970s Murano lamp with a sleek modern sofa. Drop a sculptural 1980s chair next to a clean, minimalist dining table like you've done it a thousand times. Let eras and styles chat instead of compete—no need to make it a battle of the decades.

And most important? Stay true to your own style. Just because a vintage piece is trending doesn't mean it belongs in your space.

Case in point: I almost bought a Lotus lamp, a cult-favorite vintage piece with delicate petal-like layers. It's gorgeous, but deep down, I knew it wasn't my vibe. It's like dating someone who's perfect on paper but just doesn't quite feel right. So, I went for the Jack Haywood Serpentine lamp instead—its sculptural curves and playful energy take my space to the next level.

The best vintage finds aren't about chasing hype—they're about what genuinely feels right for you and your home.

Michael shows off his collectible treasures in this colorful corner in his home studio.

Michelle and Forrest's bathroom is anything but basic. A reminder that every room deserves joy.

Where to Start If You Want More Pleasure in Your Space

If you're new to vintage, start with small, high-impact pieces that are easy to mix into your space:

- **A bold lamp—the ultimate workhorse that also moonlights as a statement piece.**
- **A funky mirror—reflects light, adds character, and never goes out of style.**
- **A unique chair—a conversation starter that doesn't need to match everything else.**
- **A cool tray or bowl—adds charm to a coffee table or kitchen counter.**

Hit up your local thrift stores, flea markets, and estate sales, or go online (Facebook Marketplace, 1stDibs, and Chairish are my faves). If you're feeling brave, set a budget and dive in with no expectations—you might just walk away with something amazing.

Future Vintage: The Pieces You'll Pass Down

The magic of vintage? It's not just about shopping—it's about curating. It's about picking pieces that will tell a story long after you're gone. One day, that piece you've been hunting for could be the very thing someone else stumbles upon and has to have.

A treasure we bring into our home today—whether it's a hand-thrown ceramic vase, a sculptural side table that steals the show, or a mirror so chic it deserves its own Instagram account—could be the future vintage item that people will fight over at an estate sale. So, when you buy, don't just grab anything; buy with intention. Look for pieces with real character, craftsmanship, and soul.

And who knows? In fifty years, that perfectly broken-in sofa you adore or the funky lamp that makes you smile could end up in someone else's home. For them, it won't just be furniture—it'll be a time capsule. A piece of history that's been passed down, keeping the story alive.

This open kitchen-living space in a previous apartment of mine uses pops of color against white walls and a checkered rug to find balance and brightness.

Vintage Moves—5 Key Takeaways

1. ENJOY THE HUNT.
The thrill is in the chase—finding those little gems feels like winning the lottery.

2. MIX IT UP.
Too much vintage? It can weigh down a space. Blend eras to keep things fresh and exciting.

3. STAY TRUE TO YOUR STYLE.
Trends come and go, but your style? It's timeless. Stick with what speaks to you.

4. PRACTICE SUSTAINABILITY.
Give vintage items a second life. Save the planet while filling your space with pieces built to last.

5. CHOOSE WITH PURPOSE.
What you buy today could be someone's future treasure.

Match the Item to Its Era

Here are six vintage finds. Can you match them to their time period? Don't worry; I'll share the answers at the end!

OPTIONS TO MATCH:

A 1980s
B 1960s
C 1950s
D 1970s
E 1990s
F 1940s

NOW, MATCH EACH PHOTO TO ITS LETTER:

1 Charles and Ray Eames—LCW Lounge Chair
(Evans Products / later Herman Miller)

2 George Nelson—Marshmallow Sofa for Herman Miller

3 Luigi Massoni—Makeup Vanity for Poltrona Frau

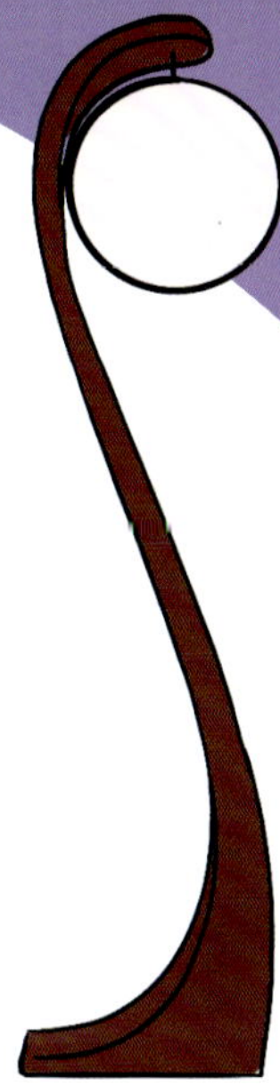

4 Jack Haywood—Serpentine Lamp

5 Ettore Sottsass—Tahiti Lamp for Memphis Milano

6 Ancona—Hummingbird Whistling Kettle

Answer Key

1 F
2 C
3 B

4 D
5 A
6 E

HOME TOUR

Michael Pybus

Artist Michael Pybus is known for his playful, thought-provoking approach to art. Mixing familiar icons, brands, and pop culture references with a dose of humor and irreverence, he creates pieces that feel both recognizable and delightfully warped. Whether he's painting, sculpting, or turning IKEA furniture showrooms into gallery installations, Michael challenges how we view consumer objects and their cultural value.

When objects and colors collide thoughtfully, magic happens. This space is a study in harmony through contrast.

Originally from Darlington in England, Michael has exhibited around the world, from London to New York and beyond. His work is part of prestigious collections, including those of Arts Council England and Takashi Murakami. In addition, he ran Welcome Screen, a home-based gallery space where he showcased emerging artists.

Michael's home, much like his art, defies expectations. It's a space that celebrates creativity, challenges norms, and stays true to his unconventional vision. His aesthetic may be eclectic, but it's also thoughtfully curated and exhaustively researched—a true reflection of his life and philosophy.

How would you describe your design aesthetic?

Time-traveling Pee-wee Herman living in the Sims.

Which items in your home would be the most coveted in a future estate sale?

By then, we'll all have uploaded our minds to the Cloud, and analogue objects will be obsolete.

If your home had a theme song, what would it be and why?

"No Good (Start the Dance)" by the Prodigy. No deep reason—it's just an absolute banger.

How does your home reflect your happiest memories?

It doesn't. My home reflects memories of what I lacked growing up. I came from a low socio-economic background, and much of my life has been defined by not having access to things and opportunities. As a kid, I would obsess over homes I saw on TV and in IKEA catalogs. When I finally could afford my own space, I mined those memories for colors, furniture, and styles. My choices are rooted in that sparse history, but now I celebrate the present by being unapologetically abundant with my aesthetic decisions—while still staying budget-conscious.

What's your favorite hidden or unexpected detail in your home that guests might overlook?

The bodies in the basement.

Are there any design "rules" you love breaking?

Outside of the laws of physics (which I can't break), rules don't factor into my design choices.

Michael expertly breaks the three-color rule every time. Cooking in this color drenched kitchen would be pure joy!

components
LIMITER
prodigy
1
2

Floral floors, a pink radiator, and punchy art turn Michael's dining nook into a storybook scene.

Michael's living room is a beautiful mash-up: earthy tones and neon, a vintage fireplace and a coral reef aquarium, and modern elements paired with classic.

How does your home reflect your childhood influences or cultural background?

Growing up in the 1980s and '90s, I was immersed in a transitional era for aesthetics and technology. Shows such as *Pee-wee's Playhouse, Saved by the Bell,* and *Clarissa Explains It All* made a lasting impact on me.

Gaming also shaped my sense of color and form—playing Mario on my NES for the first time was mind-blowing. IKEA catalogs introduced me to modern, vibrant design that felt like a revelation compared to the chintzy farmhouse style I was used to. Getting the internet in 1999 also changed everything, giving me access to a whole new world of visual inspiration.

What's your secret to scoring the best vintage or secondhand finds?

Always be on the lookout, and don't rush to buy. Be willing to wait until the price is right. Patience pays off.

Do you have a "no regrets" splurge item that instantly sparks joy?

While I'm naturally frugal, if I do splurge, I've likely done a lot of research first. One item that stands out is my Tahiti lamp by Ettore Sottsass. It's from his debut Memphis Milano collection from 1981. I'd admired it for years, and after finally gaining financial stability as an artist, I decided to buy it as a celebration of how far I'd come.

If your walls could talk, what would they say about your design journey?

My walls have signed an NDA. If they start talking, I'll see them in court.

What brands or designers do you keep coming back to when decorating your home?

IKEA, always. They consistently make great design affordable, and I appreciate their willingness to experiment with color and form. I respect how they challenge consumers with bold concepts instead of just catering to safe, generic tastes.

How do you balance function with fun in your decor?

Despite appearances, I am very practical. After all, a home is a machine for living in. Price is always a factor in my decision-making. I don't want anything in my home that stresses me out because it's more than I can afford. Makes me think of that great line from *Fight Club*: "The things that you own end up owning you."

Michael in his studio—surrounded by the creativity that fuels his colorful world.

I place value on items that are going to hold my attention long-term. It's too easy to see something on your phone and think *I have to have this new thing,* order it, and then a month later be totally indifferent about it. If I'm going to buy something, I like to do my research and sit with the idea of owning it first.

Which DIY project or personal touch in your home means the most to you?

My art studio, which is one of my bedrooms. It's crucial to have a dedicated space where I can create without barriers. Another is my coral reef aquarium—a long-term dream that finally became reality after years of research. It's a living, evolving piece that constantly engages me. It's kind of crazy to think I have a mini tropical ocean in my living room!

Animal-motif floors, smart storage, and stylish organization make Michael's studio both clever and character-filled.

IKEA
IKEA ÄLMHULT
Momsnr.: SE 55 60 74 75 51
WWW.IKEA.COM.SE/AELMHULT
10am - 8pm Monday to Friday
10am - 6pm Saturday and Sunday
Phone: + 46 77 570 05 00
0 5 2 5 9 2 1 1 2 7 9 0 1 1 2 0 1 6
SEK
ITEM # 90112790 20383
RECEIPT RUG 599,00
SUBTOTAL 599,00
Family/Business nr:
==========
599,00
TOTAL
CASH 1.000,00
POSTCODE: 34331
401,00
CHANGE DUE
ITEMS PURCHASED: 1
GST - Rate ----- Non GST -- TAX amt
A 10% 0.90 0.90
Tax invoice
Ch:2016 Tr:C06
26/03/18

Who needs traditional art when you can hang a giant IKEA receipt? Michael's bedroom feels playful and slightly irreverent.

What are some of your happy colors or color combinations?

Bubblegum pink works as a warm neutral and pairs well with just about anything. I also like juxtaposing earthy, natural tones with artificial, plastic-like hues. The key is finding the right balance so colors feel in conversation, not conflict.

Any advice for someone wanting to incorporate dopamine decor into their space?

Be mindful of why you want dopamine decor—is it genuinely your taste or just a reaction to what you see online? Don't let social media dictate your aesthetic. Instead, seek inspiration from diverse sources like films, books, nature, and art. Cultivate a style that's authentically yours, rather than one shaped by fleeting trends.

Unexpected touches, like a green tub and whimsical tiles, make Michael's bathroom surreal in the best way.

Michael's DOPAMENU

• APPETIZERS •

Draw inspiration from technology and gaming for your home design.

Mix earthy colors with plastic-like hues.

• MAINS •

Be patient with items on your vintage decor wish list—wait till the price is right.

Do your research before making a purchase and only buy decor that you'll appreciate years down the line. Ditch impulsive, trend-based buying.

• DESSERT •

Have a coral reef aquarium in your living room.

HOME TOUR

Lizzy Plapinger

(aka LPX)

When it comes to blending music, art, and fearless self-expression, Lizzy Plapinger—better known as LPX—does it with energy and style. Whether she's creating music, curating her eclectic wardrobe, or transforming her Brooklyn apartment into a visual masterpiece, Lizzy approaches everything with a sense of bold, joyful rebellion.

Lizzy's living room has layers of primary colors with white walls and graphic textiles for a space that feels bold yet balanced.

With deep roots in her native London and an impressive fifteen-year career in the music industry, Lizzy has always been fueled by her passion for color, movement, and breaking boundaries. As the co-founder of Neon Gold Records and one half of the alt electro-pop duo MS MR, she's shaped not just her own artistic identity but also the soundscape of modern indie pop. Now with her solo project, LPX, Lizzy's creativity spills over into her living space, where vibrant hues and unconventional pieces reflect her dynamic spirit.

Every corner of Lizzy's home is a visual anthem of spontaneity and unfiltered expression. Her unapologetically extra space is a tribute to living with intention and joy, proving that when you embrace your instincts, your home becomes a dynamic canvas of personal evolution.

How would you describe your design aesthetic?

I call it "Pantone Punk"—a maximalist, color-forward aesthetic rooted in vibrant, joyful rebellion. I'm inspired by design movements like Bauhaus, Memphis, op art, and art deco, but more than anything, I see myself as a colorist. My style is all about blending the highbrow and lowbrow, the silly and the sublime, and the found and the crafted.

Which Items in your home would be the most coveted in a future estate sale?

Definitely my curated closet—it's an evolving collection of vintage pieces from all over the world. My hand-painted furniture, especially my dresser, would also make the list. And my most prized possession? A vintage Guggenheim Kandinsky-style rug.

If your home had a soundtrack what would it be and why?

Thunder, Lightning, Strike by the Go! Team is probably my favorite album of all time and perfectly captures the vibe I hope my space conveys. It's casually high-octane and inviting while seamlessly mixing genres. I love its warm, fizzy, familiar yet fresh energy. I feel like in an alternate universe, the album could have been made in my apartment.

What was once a pass-through is now a joyful dressing room. A DIY dresser, hand-painted mirror, and color-trimmed door bring major character into a compact footprint. Black-and-white checks ground the look, letting bold hues pop.

Impossible to miss (or forget), the oversized [illegible] pillow brings pure whimsy in Lizzy's living room. Her hand-painted coffee table, cabinet, and art make the space feel deeply expressive and wildly off-script.

Lizzy's kitchen feels lived-in, loved, and fully hers—doodles, snapshots, and pops of color tell a rich story.

MSMR
MSMR
Lunar Phase Calendar
2025
Color-aid

How does your home reflect your happiest memories?

My home is like a living scrapbook of my creative journey. From mementos like TV cards from MS MR performances on Fallon and Letterman to the neon sign from Neon Gold's legendary club nights, every piece has a story. My studio, which is part of my apartment, serves as both a reflection of my past and a chrysalis for future ideas.

What's your favorite hidden or unexpected detail in your home that guests might overlook?

My chromatic soft sculpture palm tree by Jeff and Lisa Wright. Despite being bold and colorful, it somehow blends into the vibrant backdrop. It's quirky, unexpected, and perfectly at home here.

Lizzy's hand-painted dresser is a fan favorite—and it's easy to see why. It's a one-of-a-kind explosion of color, joy, and creative energy.

Lizzy, surrounded by her vivid creations in her studio.

Are there any design "rules" you love breaking?

I don't care for neutrals, especially beige. Instead, I lean into silver, chrome, or bold patterns like black-and-white ones as my version of a neutral.

How does your home reflect your childhood influences or cultural background?

Growing up in London shaped my love for vintage finds. My mom ran a small business selling antiques, and I inherited her passion. I used to accompany her to huge antique fairs, and I fell in love with hunting down unique pieces. By the time I was a teenager, I was a fixture at the Portobello Market on weekends. Later, as I toured the world, I was able to take my passion for vintage finds to a whole other level. Now my closet and apartment are like an ever-evolving charm bracelet representing my travels.

What's your secret to scoring the best vintage or secondhand finds?

I'm *always* looking. Online and in real life. Wherever I am, I like to introduce myself to sellers and store owners—that way, when a special piece that fits my distinct style shows up, they'll think of me.

Since current trends lean more minimal and neutral, lots of spectacular, quirky, avant-garde, maximalist, and color-forward pieces are getting ignored. It's kind of the perfect time to score great deals and pieces.

Do you have a "no regrets" splurge item that instantly sparks joy?

My vintage Alessi chrome tea kettle. It's my daily beacon of beauty, sitting on my stove like a perfect piece of functional sculpture. It's unhinged how much I love it, especially the star stopper whistler.

If your walls could talk, what would they say about your design journey?

I've been lucky to always love where I live and have the ability to turn every place I've inhabited into a home—even my college dorm rooms. My style has always been playful and colorful, but over the years my creativity has evolved to become more articulate and ambitious. There's an audaciousness and a lack of preciousness now about playing on a bigger scale that feels really exciting.

What brands or designers do you keep coming back to when decorating your home?

Zander Schlacter. His unique, playful designs feel in tune with my aesthetic, and I admire how his pieces complement my painted furniture.

Who says bedrooms have to be moody and serene? Lizzy dials up the color in hers with bold primary colors and attention-grabbing art.

OPEN SOCRATES
AGNES CALLARD
SECOND PLACE
RACHEL CUSK
CHEAPER FASTER BETTER
TOM STEYER

How do you balance function with fun in your decor?

I keep the number of items minimal, but every piece is a statement. This balance between a maximalist aesthetic and a minimalist quantity keeps the space feeling vibrant yet uncluttered.

Which DIY project or personal touch in your home means the most to you?

I have at least five hand-painted furniture pieces, my favorite being the dresser, which is the centerpiece of the apartment. I dream of one day creating an entire installation like Liza Lou's epic beaded kitchen, which took five years to make.

What are some of your happy colors or color combinations?

I *love* complementary colors. The tension between opposites makes things feel complete. I'm all about setting multiple colors against black. Black allows colors to really pop, creating a sense of illumination that feels magical.

Any advice for someone wanting to incorporate dopamine decor into their space?

Be in touch with what lights you up. It can be challenging to tune out all the noise in our world today, but it's paramount to stay connected to your instincts. Your instincts will guide you toward a space that feels singular, warm, and joyful.

Fashion gets the dopamine decor treatment too. Lizzy's DIY leather jacket pops against a statement wall of oversized sequins.

Lizzy's DOPAMENU

• APPETIZERS •

Mix highbrow with lowbrow.

Customize your furniture by hand-painting it.

• MAINS •

Keep the number of items in your home minimal, but make each item a statement piece.

Ditch beige and use silver, chrome, or black-and-white patterns as your base.

• DESSERT •

Build your vintage collection by treasure hunting at antique fairs and flea markets.

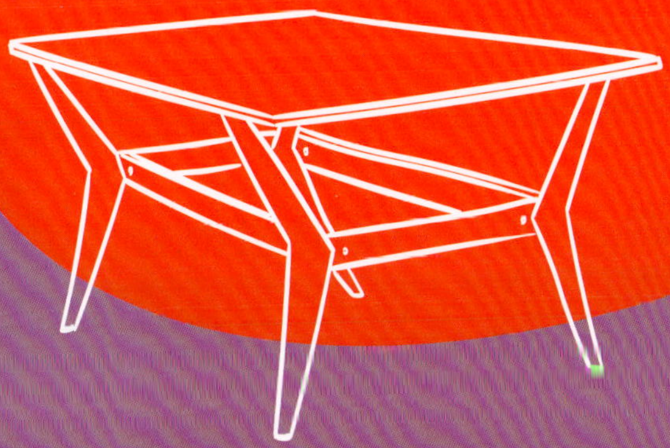

CHAPTER THREE

MOOD

Color That Hits Different

Six shades of joy greet you in the entryway of my last NYC apartment. That burst of color and the artwork (which conceals an electrical box) was always the perfect welcome home.

Mood is the vibe a space gives off. It's the way a room makes you feel before you even have a second to think about it. It's the difference between sinking into a cozy, candlelit booth that instantly relaxes you and stepping into a bright, buzzing café that fills you with energy.

And guess what? Color is the biggest mood-setter of them all.

It's wild how fast color can shift energy. Ever walked into a restaurant with deep red walls and suddenly felt a little more adventurous and ready to indulge? Or been in an all-white room that felt so stark you weren't sure if you were in a luxury boutique or a hospital waiting room? That's mood, baby. And color is the DJ, controlling the tempo.

The Science of Color and Mood

Okay, let's geek out for a second. Color affects us on a biological level. Our brains process it through the limbic system—the same part that controls emotions, memory, and motivation. That's why certain colors make you feel hyped, while others calm you down. Your body literally reacts to them. It's like when you hear your favorite song on the radio. Suddenly you're dancing in your kitchen, even if it's 7 a.m.

Dopamine is the key. It's the thing that gives you a little burst of happiness when you see something amazing, sip a delicious drink, or finally crush a goal. Dopamine says, "Hey, you're doing great—keep it up!" And that's why I think of color as its own kind of therapy (minus the copays). A red coffee maker, a pink ceiling, a vibrant fruit bowl—sometimes just glancing at a colorful object can shift your mood in an instant.

Warm colors (red, orange, yellow) tend to be energizing. They get your heart rate up, boost appetite, and make a space feel alive—which is why you often see them in restaurants. Cool colors (blue, green, purple), on the other hand, do the opposite: they slow things down, help you focus, and create a chill, relaxing vibe—think a five-star spa or that dreamy corner at your local coffee shop where you can sip your latte in peace and pretend like you've got your life together.

But here's the twist: How *you* respond to color isn't just science—it's also shaped by your experiences. One person might find a neon-green wall playful and exciting, while another might see it and think, *Not this highlighter shade ruining my peace*. That's why dopamine decor isn't about rules—it's about you.

Personally, I find that deep and moody colors don't do much to uplift my mood, so I avoid them in my home. But for some people, a dark, moody space might be the perfect retreat—a cocoon that feels safe, cozy, and intimate. A deep blue bedroom or a forest-green library could be exactly what makes them feel at home. And I do appreciate those kinds of spaces in other settings—like a bar with dim lighting, deep emerald walls, and velvet furniture. There, it feels intentional, cozy, even glamorous. But in my living room? Nah. I need a little more fun than that.

That's the thing about color: it's not just about what looks good. It's about what feels right for the space and the person living in it. And yes, neutrals are colors too. The right shade of white, gray, or beige can make all the difference, setting the stage for a space that feels warm, soft, or strikingly crisp. But in this book? Neutrals are taking a back seat. It's about bringing the bold, not the beige. Here, we're focusing on the colors that make a statement—the ones that inspire joy, shift energy, and bring a space to life.

Fearless Color: Why I Love It and How You Can Too

When I was growing up in India, bright colors weren't a choice—they were life. I saw color everywhere: in clothes, in bustling markets, at weddings, in everyday moments. My culture taught me to lean into color rather than fear it. While in the West, minimalism and neutral palettes were seen as the height of sophistication (aka the "If it's not beige or gray—or better yet, *greige*—is it even aesthetic?" phase), in India, color was woven into every part of life. It wasn't something to be cautious about or used sparingly; it was meant to be embraced.

(Except for pastels, that is. They weren't a big thing for me at that point since everything around me was so vibrant and saturated . . . but we'll get to that.)

Shopping for clothes as a kid, I remember my aunt always buying the same fabric in two different colors—one for my cousin and one for me. We got to pick our own, and I usually went for the louder, brighter option, like bold red or sunny yellow, while my cousin leaned toward navy or deep green. Looking back, that was probably my first experience with color as a form of self-expression. I wasn't just choosing clothes—I was making a statement about who I was.

Though I'm more spiritual than religious these days, I grew up in a Hindu family, where white was reserved for funerals and bright colors were worn for weddings. If you've ever been to an Indian wedding, you get it. It's color overload in the best way possible: red, pink, green, yellow, orange—every shade signals joy, festivity, and celebration.

This 1990s toucan lamp is one of my favorite vintage finds. Here it sits on a chair I built in a furniture-making class, and jazzed up with a signature color pop.

London and the Magic of Pastels

Pastels weren't exactly off my radar—they just weren't my thing. I wore some softer shades like light blue or buttery yellow, but I wasn't drawn to them the way I was to bold, high-energy colors. And I definitely wasn't a *pink girlie*. While plenty of girls grow up loving soft pastel or candy pink, I was all about fuchsia—that deep, electric pink that felt confident and celebratory. But then I moved to London, and suddenly, pastels weren't just delicate; they were powerful.

Strolling through Chelsea, I saw color in a whole new way—not just as individual shades but as combinations that felt unexpectedly perfect together. You might love two colors separately, like yellow and lilac, but when paired, they create something even more magical.

This world of color pairings opened up to me as I explored the architecture and painted facades of London. I also started noticing how colors play off each other in sequence—not just in a single space, but as you move through a home.

A lack of walls didn't stop me from giving this NYC apartment the full dopamine decor treatment. I added color to the ceiling, a bold rug underfoot, and plenty of fun furniture.

In interiors, this is called *enfilade*—when a series of rooms align, allowing you to see one through another. The way colors connect from room to room can be just as impactful as the colors themselves. You can create beauty by using distinct shades in each space, but when viewed together, the colors feel like they're in conversation.

Incorporating pastels into my home became my way of softening the space without losing the joy that brighter colors offered. They weren't a compromise between neutrals and bold colors—they were their own mood. I discovered Danish Pastel, a style where neutral tones form the base of the space, while pastels—like blush, mint, and lavender—show up in key decor elements like throw pillows, rugs, and furniture. To add a punch of energy, bold accents—think cobalt blue vases or deep green lamps—make up around 10 percent of the palette. This blend of soft pastels with vibrant pops of color creates a balanced, playful atmosphere without feeling overly sweet. It became my perfect bridge between minimalism and maximalism, proving that pastels can pack just as much of a punch as brights when used thoughtfully.

Where to Start If You're Afraid of Color

One thing I hear all the time on social media? "I want to use color, but I don't know where to start."

Two words: Start small.

A bold sofa in a neutral space. A vibrant lamp. A colorful piece of art. And if you're still unsure, start with colors you love wearing. If you love how you feel in a cobalt sweater or a pink dress, chances are you'll also love those colors in your space.

Paint is one of the easiest, least expensive ways to add color. And if you don't love it? Here's a hot tip: You can always paint over it.

I've had my share of regrets—like the time I painted an IKEA cabinet fluorescent yellow instead of a softer, buttery yellow. Did I hate it? Yes. But I learned. And the beauty of paint is, with one coat of primer and two coats of a new color, you can reinvent anything.

Speaking of primer, let's debunk the biggest color myth: Once you paint a wall a bright color, you can never go back to white. False. One coat of primer, two coats of paint, and boom—back to neutral if you want.

I've even gone viral on social media showing how I turned my colorful rental walls back to white, proving that with a good primer and a couple coats of paint, no color choice is ever truly permanent. Color commitment? Pfft, more like color tryouts.

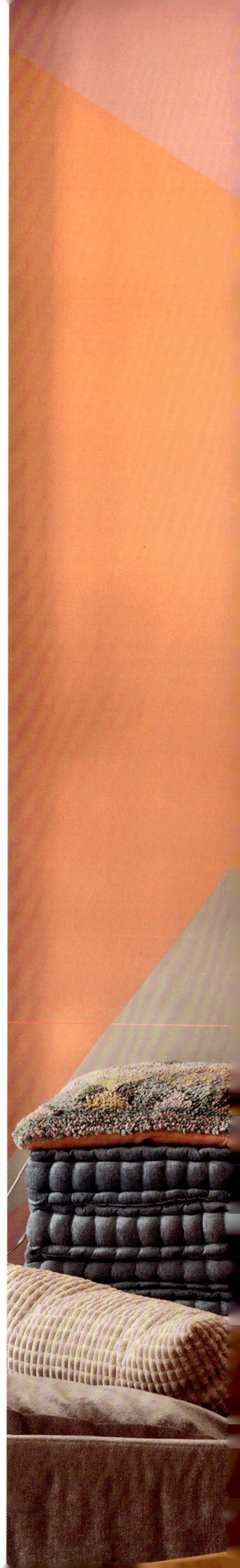

A hand-painted mural, in earthy brights, turns Averie's TV wall into art. Add disco balls and a rattan chair, and boom—the mood is set to max.

How to Build a Color Palette

Let's talk strategy. A common mistake? Focusing on one color without thinking about the bigger picture. Sure, you might love saffron yellow, but does it play nice with your rug? Your furniture? The room next door?

Colors don't exist in isolation. When you move through your home, you see multiple spaces at once—through doorways, down hallways, across open layouts. That's where color flow (or sight lines) comes in. The goal isn't to make every room match but to create a connection between them. Maybe the soft lilac in your bedroom reappears as an accent in your living room, or the deep blue of your hallway complements the green in your kitchen. Make it a family reunion, not a competition.

Building a cohesive color palette is like putting together a great outfit—each piece should work with the others, even if it stands out on its own. For most people, that means choosing shades that complement each other, creating a flow from one room to the next.

But some designers and artists lean into contrast, purposely clashing colors to create something bold and unexpected. And if mixing wild, high-contrast colors gives you a dopamine boost? Then you do you. Color is personal, and the best palettes are the ones that make you feel something. Trust your gut—if you love the clash, let it happen.

My hand-painted mirror in red and pink—forever my favorite combo—adds instant charm to an everyday corner.

STEP 1: START WITH A BASE

Pick a color you know you love—something you won't get tired of seeing every day. This could be a soft pink, sky blue, pistachio green, or lilac. Think of it as the foundation of your palette. Like that one perfect lip gloss you can't stop reaching for—smooth, reliable, and always on point. Or your favorite jeans, the ones that fit just right and make you feel like you can conquer the world.

STEP 2: LAYER IN ACCENTS

Now add complementary colors for depth and contrast. Accent colors make a space feel intentional instead of random. Little pops of red, cobalt blue, or emerald green work really well as accents on lighter or pastel colors, creating a striking contrast without overwhelming the space. Some color pairings are easy and always work, while others take more finesse. Experiment and see what feels right.

For me, certain combinations feel effortless—like pink and red or green and blue. But some pairings are trickier. Neons, for example, are tough to integrate unless they're balanced by softer shades. Lime green with rusty orange? Love it in a design magazine, but in my own home? Too intense. Other combinations that need more thought: brown and green (can feel heavy), red and black (too harsh), or green and yellow (can skew cartoonish if the shades aren't just right). It's like matchmaking, but with colors.

If you're unsure, start with two colors that feel natural together, then add a third that complements both. From there, introduce a fourth. Over time, you'll develop a formula that works for you.

STEP 3: TEST AND ADJUST

Start small—a colorful pillow, an accent wall, or a statement chair. See how the colors interact in different lighting. If the balance feels off, tweak it. A great palette isn't built overnight—it's something you refine over time. Like your favorite recipe: taste, adjust, add a little spice. Don't skip the salt!

How I Built My Palette

When I was designing the living room in my last Brooklyn apartment, the first thing I knew for sure was that I wanted a pink ceiling. I already owned a pink sofa, so I knew these two elements had to anchor the space.

From there, I started layering in colors. I found a multicolored rug with shades of yellow, sky blue, and lilac—it balanced the pink and added contrast. Then came my kitchen island. I knew that pink and green work beautifully together (pink and green is like the *yass* moment of color combos . . . instant chef's kiss!), so I used peel-and-stick tiles to transform it into a gorgeous shade of dark green. For the barstools, I introduced rust. While rust and lime can be a risky pair, rust and deep green work really well together. Rust and pink can also be an unexpectedly great pairing. Looking at the space from a distance, I saw green, rust, and pink blend seamlessly—even though I had added them at different times. That's the thing about color: it evolves, but if you're thoughtful about how each new shade connects to the ones already in place, it all comes together.

That's also why I love experimenting with unexpected combinations. One of my boldest color moments was a collaboration with Benjamin Moore, where in my entryway, I combined bright red with vibrant green and lilac—plus a few other shades—pulling inspiration from a Japanese book on color theory.

Honestly? I wasn't sure how it would turn out. And apparently, neither were you guys. When Benjamin Moore reposted my video, the comments were filled with people begging me to reconsider—"Girl, don't do it!"—followed by a collective "Wait . . . WOW" when the final product was revealed.

Even I had a moment of doubt. The colors were so outside my usual comfort zone. But you know what? Sometimes you've just got to trust the process. And when I stepped back? The combination was electric. Every time I opened the door to my apartment, I was greeted by this colorful burst of energy—something that instantly signaled, "You're home! You're in your happy place!" And that's the magic of color—it can surprise you, push you, and make a space feel completely unique.

This Ancona hummingbird kettle was a hard-won eBay score. Now, it's proudly perched in my kitchen.

Sculptural and distinctive, Yinka Ilori's fruit bowl, a tulip taper holder, and a honeybee coaster perk up this marble moment.

Sometimes the best palettes aren't the safest ones. They're the ones that make you stop and go, "I never would have thought of that, but it *works*."

Some classic pairings I personally love:

PINK + RED
(BOLD AND PLAYFUL)

GREEN + PINK
(WORKS EVERY TIME)

GREEN + BLUE
(EARTHY AND GROUNDED)

YELLOW + PEACHY PINK
(WARM AND INVITING)

MINT + LILAC
(SOFT AND WHIMSICAL)

RED + LILAC
(ROMANTIC AND STRIKING)

YELLOW + LILAC
(UNEXPECTED BUT BEAUTIFUL)

ORANGE + PINK
(CHEERFUL AND LIVELY)

Finding Your Own Formula

Paint isn't just decoration—it's basically a mood in a can. And your walls? They're the ultimate mood board. Whether you're layering in bold shades or experimenting with pastels, the key is to approach color with intention. You might love a certain shade, but does it work with your furniture, your rug, or even the next room over? The way colors interact shapes the experience of your home, making the difference between a space that feels curated and one that feels disjointed.

But that doesn't mean you have to play it safe. Some of the best color moments happen in unexpected places—ceilings, cabinet knobs, kitchen appliances, exposed columns, even mirrors. A painted ceiling can transform a space, turning what's usually overlooked into a statement. I've done it in my own apartment, where floor-to-ceiling glass left little room for wall color, and in a client's home, where wallpaper on the ceiling added a dramatic touch.

My relationship with color has evolved over time. I once leaned into saturated hues, then shifted to pastels, and now I embrace both. The entryway in my last apartment burst with six or seven bold colors for an instant jolt of joy, while my living room's pink ceiling created a calming effect. It's all about balance—finding the right mix that makes a space feel good to live in.

Some of my biggest color lessons have come from trial and error.

Using multiple shades of the same color—like bright red, deep red, and burgundy—can create depth and dimension. Layering colors is like stacking pancakes; sometimes more syrup is the secret. But, like, don't drown them. A little goes a long way.

And not every experiment works. Like that neon yellow IKEA cabinet I'll never forget. But that's okay—I donated it (you know what they say about one girl's trash . . .), though I could have just repainted it with that magic primer trick. Another cabinet I painted vibrant pink and added checkered knobs. That piece became a favorite. The beauty of color is that it's never permanent—you can always repaint, swap, or rework it until it feels right.

If you're still nervous about using color, remember to breathe deep and start small: a bold accent chair, a colorful vase, or a painted door. And if you're unsure how a color will feel in your space, there are plenty of tools to help—apps that let you visualize colors together and paint brand features that preview how a shade will look in a room. Most important, trust your instincts. Color is personal—what feels like a risk to someone else might be exactly what makes *your* space feel like home.

At the end of the day, a space can be calming or joyful, sophisticated or playful. But what makes it truly special is the color you bring into it—and the confidence to make it your own.

Michael's entryway bursts with art and saturated hues—a reminder that adult spaces can be just as lively as a kid's room.

Color Moves—5 Key Takeaways

1. PRESS THE RESET BUTTON WITH PRIMER.
A coat of primer plus two coats of fresh paint can erase any color misstep.

2. THINK OF PASTELS AS NEUTRALS.
Pastels are like beige but with more personality—an easy gateway into color.

3. START SMALL.
A bold accent piece lets you experiment before committing.

4. BUILD A COHESIVE PALETTE.
Pick a base, layer in accents, and make sure shades complement each other.

5. SURPRISE YOURSELF.
Ceilings, mirrors, exposed columns—unexpected pops of color make the biggest impact.

LEFT A hand-painted cabinet and custom palm tree make this corner of Lizzy's home unforgettable—books and lighting styled to perfection.
RIGHT This faux cake turns a basic tissue box into a sweet design surprise.

Color Personality Quiz

Find Your Dopamine Decor Color Palette

Ever wonder what your ideal color palette says about you? This fun, quick quiz is designed to decode your design vibe and point you toward a color story that sparks joy every time you walk through the door. Ready to meet your match?

QUESTIONS

1. What's your ideal Saturday?

- **A** A spa day with candles and calming music
- **B** Brunch with friends at a buzzy café
- **C** Wandering through an art museum or exploring a new city
- **D** Cozying up with a book in your favorite chair

2. How do you want your home to feel?

- **A** Serene and peaceful
- **B** Bright and full of life
- **C** Chic and sophisticated
- **D** Warm and inviting

3. Pick a texture you'd want in every room:

- **A** Fluffy sheepskin
- **B** Glossy lacquer
- **C** Smooth marble
- **D** Woven rattan

4. What speaks to you the most?

- A A soft, cloud-like lilac sweater
- B A punchy tangerine handbag
- C A deep green velvet sofa
- D A rustic mustard-colored throw blanket

5. What's your ideal art piece?

- A A minimalist line drawing
- B An abstract color explosion
- C A moody landscape photograph
- D Folk-inspired textile art

YOUR RESULTS

Mostly As *Muted & Minimalist*
Soft grays, dusty lilacs, warm taupes. You're all about calm, control, and quiet beauty.

Mostly Bs *Vibrant & Expressive*
Cobalt, tangerine, hot pink. You're a maximalist at heart and thrive in color-rich environments that make you feel alive.

Mostly Cs *Dark & Dramatic*
Inky blues, deep greens, and moody maroons. You love elegance, intimacy, and design that tells a slow-burning story.

Mostly Ds *Earthy & Eclectic*
Rust, ocher, sage green. Your style is layered, cozy, and full of vintage soul.

HOME TOUR

Averie Cole

Averie Cole is an artist and photographer whose home is more than a living space—it's a dynamic, creative studio where art, community, and well-being seamlessly come together. Originally from Sydney, Australia, and now based in Jersey City, New Jersey, Averie takes a fearless, joyful approach to creativity that defines both her work and her lively, lived-in home.

Averie's view from the living room peeks into her pink kitchen and bar drenched in charm and color.

No wall left behind. Averie brings unexpected flair to a bedroom door with another one of her signature murals.

Averie's apartment is filled with hand-painted murals, bold textiles, and personal artwork. Whether she's photographing portraits, quilting, hosting community dinners, or simply reimagining her space, Averie infuses every detail with intention and personality.

An ever-evolving canvas filled with personality, creativity, and warmth, her home is all about living boldly and celebrating the things that make life joyful.

How would you describe your design aesthetic?

Colorful, lived-in, and joy-fueled. I'm all about bold color, big personality, and layering things that tell a story. I love mixing vintage pieces with personal art and unexpected details. I want every corner to feel like it has a pulse—alive with memory and intention, but never too serious. I'd call it a little bit maximalist, a little bit nostalgic, and completely me.

Which items in your home would be the most coveted in a future estate sale?

Definitely my Mud Witch mugs—they always get comments. My quilts would be up there too; they're all handmade, slow-stitched with love, and each one tells its own story. The two paintings by my friend Rebecca above my dining table would definitely be in the running—they're the soul of the apartment. And probably the ombré pink coffee mug stand I rescued from the street; it's got main character energy now.

If your home had a theme song, what would it be and why?

"Juice" by Lizzo. It's bright, confident, funky, and fun—just like my apartment. I like to think my home throws a little party for your senses the moment you walk in.

How does your home reflect your happiest memories?

My happiest memories are tied to color, creativity, connection, and community—and my home reflects all of that. The art on my walls isn't just decoration; it's layered with meaning. Most of it was made by people I love—friends, my sister, even my son. One of my closest friends gave me a painting during a transformative time, and it still greets me when I walk through the door. My son's drawings are tucked into corners throughout the space, keeping it playful and full of heart.

Averie's dining nook is filled with special personal touches, like artwork by a friend. A masterclass in bringing color to a neutral base.

My home is also where I create, work, and gather. I love hosting friends for dinners, exhibitions, and creative meet-ups. It's a space that feels welcoming, warm, and alive with possibility. Designing it to function as both a studio and a living space has pushed me to stay intentional and creative with how everything flows. It's not about perfection—it's about energy, warmth, and the feeling that you belong here.

Open shelving and renter-friendly peel-and-stick wallpaper on the fridge elevates this everyday kitchen to extraordinary.

What's your favorite hidden or unexpected detail in your home that guests might overlook?

Probably the checkerboard wall in my bedroom. The room doesn't have windows and has high ceilings, so I color-drenched it in soft peach tones and added a hand-painted checker pattern for warmth and movement. It's subtle, but it completely transformed the space from cold to cozy.

Another favorite is the little gym setup tucked into the bedroom. I spray-painted some of the equipment pink so it blends in—it's my happy corner: strong, soft, and colorful all at once.

Are there any design "rules" you love breaking?

All of them. I've painted every wall in this rental—even the ceilings. I mix bold patterns with bold colors, hang art higher or lower than expected, and definitely don't believe in "less is more." If it makes me happy, it stays—even if it clashes. Especially if it clashes.

How does your home reflect your childhood influences or cultural background?

Growing up in Australia, I was surrounded by creativity, nature, and a casual chaos that feels very present in my home today. It's relaxed, tactile, and filled with handmade things. As a kid, I'd rearrange rooms, draw on walls (sorry, Mum), and make little zones for myself. That instinct to create a world within four walls never left me.

What's your secret to scoring the best vintage or secondhand finds?

Trash day in my building—seriously. People throw out incredible stuff. My rattan furniture and mug stand both came from there. I also stalk Facebook Marketplace and keep notifications on for specific items. The secret? Not being afraid of a little grime or DIY—spray paint fixes everything.

Do you have a "no regrets" splurge item that instantly sparks joy?

My Mud Witch mug collection. The mugs are handmade, colorful, and a little weird, and using them makes having my coffee feel like a ritual. I also splurged on custom-cut glass to restore the rattan furniture I found. It felt like a big commitment at the time, but I love it—it was worth every penny.

If your walls could talk, what would they say about your design journey?

They'd say, "She was scared at first—but look at her now." I used to worry about getting it wrong, but now I paint with confidence, trust my gut, and experiment. My walls might also say, "Please, no more paint," but they'd say it with love.

Averie's rattan bookshelf was a trash-day find, now repurposed and revived as a living room gem that doubles as a room divider for her son's space. That rattan coffee table? Also a rescue.

Averie's hallway to the bathroom is a feast of color, art, and distinctive shapes.

What brands or designers do you keep coming back to when decorating your home?

I love offbeat pieces that feel full of character. Coming Soon in New York City is a favorite. Most of the art in my space comes from friends or people I know personally—it makes everything feel more meaningful.

How do you balance function with fun in your decor?

I choose pieces that make me smile but still serve a purpose. Like colorful baskets that hide toys or quilts that are both art and practical. I love the idea that everyday things can be beautiful too.

Which DIY project or personal touch in your home means the most to you?

Quilting. I taught myself during the pandemic, inspired by a friend back home in Australia who's an award-winning quilter. Quilting is slow and meditative and feels deeply personal. Each one is a little legacy piece that's both cozy and functional.

What are some of your happy colors or color combinations?

Pink, always. I love mixing shades of pink with sunny oranges, warm neutrals, and pops of mint or cobalt. My favorite combos feel a little sun-bleached—like memories of a perfect summer day.

Any advice for someone wanting to incorporate dopamine decor into their space?

Start small and follow your gut. Your home should feel like a hug when you walk in—not a showroom. If it makes you happy, it belongs there.

Averie in her vibrant, personality-packed home.

Averie's DOPAMENU

• APPETIZERS •

Spray-paint gym equipment or other non-aesthetic functional pieces so they blend in with the rest of your decor.

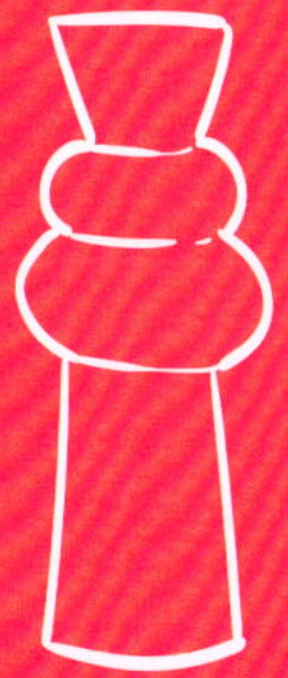

Rescue items from the trash and give them a new life.

• MAINS •

Add hand-painted murals to your walls to bring in personality and movement.

Hang meaningful art made by friends and family in unexpected places.

• DESSERT •

Build a colorful coffee mug collection to brighten your morning routine.

HOME TOUR

Michelle Norris & Forrest Aguar

Michelle Norris and Forrest Aguar are a creative duo whose home is a vibrant blend of eclectic influences, personal art, and playful design. Based in Atlanta, Georgia, they've transformed their industrial loft into a colorful, inviting space that balances bold patterns, artistic expression, and thoughtful curation.

Michelle and Forrest's living room is a joyful paradise. The hot pink velvet sofa brings the drama, their pup brings the charm, and the clever, hand-carved coffee table brings the conversation.

With backgrounds in photography and a shared love for travel, Michelle and Forrest draw inspiration from art deco, tropical modernism, and the works of iconic architects like Luis Barragán and Ricardo Bofill. Their home brings together unexpected details, texture, and personal stories in a charming mix.

It's a space where artistic instincts guide design choices, proving that a home can be both eclectic and intentional when you follow your gut.

How would you describe your design aesthetic?

Bright, bold, and eclectic. We love mixing art deco, tropical modernism, and colorful maximalism, creating a lively, layered look that feels joyful and expressive.

Which items in your home would be the most coveted in a future estate sale?

Definitely our coffee table, which is a carved wooden sculpture of a woman—it's an absolute showstopper and was handcrafted by a local Atlanta artist. It's the most commented-on piece and truly feels like the centerpiece of our home.

If your home had a theme song, what would it be and why?

"Yellow Submarine" by the Beatles. It's whimsical, it's colorful, and it feels both playful and sophisticated—just like our space.

How does your home reflect your happiest memories?

Our home is filled with art made by our friends and by us, reminding us of creativity, community, and collaboration. We've hosted everything from dinner parties to group painting sessions, so it's a space shaped by the people we love and the moments we've shared.

What's your favorite hidden or unexpected detail in your home that guests might overlook?

Our coffee table's hidden feature—the boobs open up as doors! It's quirky and surprising, and it never fails to make people laugh.

Pops of pink, chartreuse, and teal come alive in the kitchen—it's bright, cheerful, and effortlessly layered.

Their bedroom blends texture, color, pattern, and cute pup vibes with a beautiful wooden bedframe, handmade by Forrest.

Michelle and Forrest's stylish kitchen is an exuberant blend of plants, saturated shades, and eclectic art.

Are there any design "rules" you love breaking?

We love mixing patterns and bold colors in unconventional ways. Sometimes they clash, but if it makes us happy, it stays. We also break the rule that you need formal training to be an interior designer—we've taken on projects just by trusting our instincts and love for design.

How does your home reflect your childhood influences or cultural backgrounds?

Michelle grew up loving bright colors and playful patterns—a taste that hasn't changed much since childhood. Forrest's love for art deco comes from his parents' style, while his discovery of Memphis Design later in life added a surrealist twist. Our home blends these influences into something uniquely ours.

Michelle and Forrest at home with their rescue pup, Taco.

Drenched in teal and pink, their bathroom is equal parts serene and striking.

What's your secret to scoring the best vintage or secondhand finds?

For Michelle, it's exploring antique shops in small Southern towns—unexpected treasures are always tucked away. Forrest's tip? If you see something one-of-a-kind while traveling, just buy it—you'll figure out the logistics later!

Do you have a "no regrets" splurge item that instantly sparks joy?

Our color-blocked dining chairs. They were a bit of an investment, but they're beautifully made and add a vibrant, unique touch to the room. They took sixteen months to arrive, but they were worth the wait!

If your walls could talk, what would they say about your design journey?

They'd say, "Everything happened fast." We painted the entire apartment with friends in just a few days—it was chaotic, creative, and totally worth it.

What brands or designers do you keep coming back to when decorating your home?

Zander Schlacter, Tarta Gelatina, Floyd, and Silt Studio. We also love finding unique pieces from Ukrainian design studios like OITO.

How do you balance function with fun in your decor?

We're big on practical pieces that still make us smile. For functional items, we invest in well-designed, durable pieces or go the custom-made route. Splurging where it counts—like on our sleek, stylish Haiku ceiling fans—ensures that our space stays both beautiful and practical.

What DIY project or personal touch in your home means the most to you?

Michelle's favorite is a wooden fish she found at an antique shop and painted with playful patterns—it's one of a kind and adds a personal touch to the bathroom. Forrest's favorite is the bed slats he designed and had custom-made, turning a basic frame into something unique and colorful.

BOSCH

Smart furniture placement and vibrant hues carve cozy corners into an open-concept space.

What are some of your happy colors or color combinations?

Chartreuse paired with dark blue, light pink, and dark green—it's a combination that feels fresh and balanced. We also love red and yellow together for their bold, almost nostalgic feel.

Any advice for someone wanting to incorporate dopamine decor into their space?

Start small—like with an accent wall. It's less overwhelming and makes a big impact. Or just dive in—don't worry about what others think. Color is a way to make your space feel more alive. And a small, cute dog is also essential.

This pink balcony pops against the sunny Atlanta sky—a dreamy spot for sunset hangs and recharging.

Michelle & Forrest's DOPAMENU

• APPETIZERS •

Incorporate showstopping and conversation-starting custom-made furniture and accessories.

Use clashing patterns and colors if it makes you happy.

• MAINS •

Turn painting your walls into a group activity by inviting your friends over to help you.

Mix design aesthetics to create a layered, visually rich space.

• DESSERT •

Love something you see on your travels? Buy it—and worry about how you'll bring it back later.

CHAPTER FOUR

MOVEMENT

Playing with Lighting, Texture & Pattern

My DIY disco pendant lights catch golden hour just right—a little sparkle therapy for the soul.

When it comes to designing a space that makes you feel your best, movement is the secret sauce. And no, I'm not suggesting your sofa break into the latest viral TikTok dance (although if it does, definitely film it). Movement in your home is about creating energy and vibrancy through how light, texture, and patterns interact. Movement is the heartbeat of a space, keeping it from feeling stagnant or boring.

Think of it this way: Just like a great playlist can shift your mood, movement in your space can flip the vibe from blah to brilliant.

Why Movement Matters

A space that *moves* is one that feels active, alive, and full of personality. Think about the way sunlight shifts across your favorite room, a textured fabric stops you in your tracks, or a hypnotic pattern pulls you in. When they come together just right, lighting, texture, and patterns make your space feel layered, interesting, and joyful. Keeping movement in mind as you design means creating a space that's not just seen but felt—like it's giving you a little wink every time you step inside.

The Dopamine Connection

Movement can improve the aesthetics of your space, for sure, but what's even more important is the way it makes you feel. When light bounces off a disco ball or shimmers through a stained-glass suncatcher, it triggers a burst of dopamine. Similarly, the tactile pleasure of running your hands over a textured surface or the visual thrill of a bold pattern can give you a serotonin boost. Movement brings your space to life, like blasting your favorite song and instantly feeling the vibe shift, giving it a rhythm that keeps you feeling engaged and inspired. When your surroundings feel dynamic, so do you. That's why designing for movement is designing for happiness.

Light as a Mood Booster

Light is one of the most effective (and easiest!) ways to infuse movement into your space. And the best part? Natural light—which is hands-down the best kind of light, IMO—is available to everyone, like a little gift from the sun. You don't have to pay for it, set it up, or even think about it; it's just there, waiting for you (or your ray-worshipping pug) to bask in it.

Natural light changes throughout the day, shifting from bright and energizing in the morning to soft and warm at the golden hour. It's a built-in mood booster, especially if you're lucky enough to have windows that catch those dreamy sunset vibes. My last apartment featured floor-to-ceiling windows that faced southwest, which meant I got to experience some truly incredible sunsets. The light moved through my space in waves—bright and golden one moment, then fading to deep orange and pink. Ari loved it too—he would stretch out in the sun's path, blissed-out. There's something about those shifting colors that makes everything feel more special.

Lighting can seriously impact your mood and your daily habits. But what if you don't get a ton of natural light? Not every space is blessed with panoramic windows and technicolor sunsets, but you don't need to be limited by the confines of your space. Sometimes you just have to get a little creative and make your own light. Try adding string lights around mirrors or reflective objects near windows to bounce whatever light you do get around the room.

In one of my old apartments, my windows faced northeast and were partially blocked by big trees. On cloudy days, the lack of light could make my space feel downright gloomy. I didn't enjoy cooking in that apartment at all because the kitchen—being the area farthest from the windows—was always so dim. In contrast, my last apartment's kitchen was filled with light, and I found myself cooking way more.

When you start filling your space with light, whether natural or artificial, remember to think beyond the basic: table lamps instead of overhead lights, clusters of candles for that flickering glow, strip lights to add a soft edge, or even backlit headboards to bring ambience to your bedroom. Rather than relying on one light source, layer in small ones to make your space feel intentional and warm.

In my bedroom, I have a little lamp on each nightstand. There's just enough light to read a book before bed without killing my calm. I also love using adjustable lights for compact spaces—a pendant light over a dining table that can be pulled up or down depending on whether you're eating solo or hosting friends. A task lamp that can be pointed in different directions is also a game-changer when space is tight.

One of my favorite times of day is when I turn on all the ambient lights in my living room in the evening. It's like flipping the switch from day to night—the soft, calming light signals that it's time to unwind. I've collected a few fun lamps over the years, including some vintage finds, and I love turning them on when the sun sets. No harsh overheads—just a glow that makes the space feel instantly more relaxed.

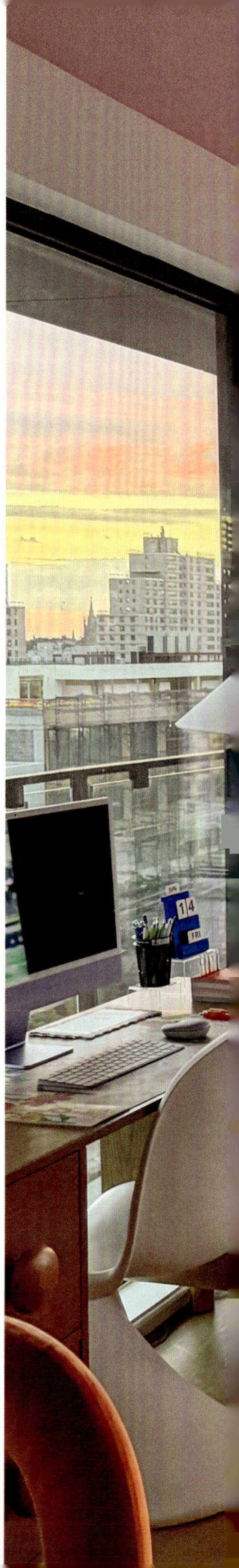

Sunset magic and dopamine glow—this golden moment in my NYC living room is pure joy.

DREAM BABY DREAM
Color Me Floral

Old meets new in this room where modern shapes mingle with a traditional fireplace—unexpected and unforgettable.

Smart Lighting Vibes

When it comes to making your own light, we've thankfully leveled up from the old-school, harsh tube lights I grew up with in India. (Those lights were cold, flat, and about as inviting as a hospital waiting room.) Now? We've got endless options to create exactly the vibe we want.

I'm a big fan of smart lighting, which you can adjust and control from the ease and comfort of your phone. It's like the decor equivalent of switching your phone from light mode to dark mode—adaptable, effortless, and always on point. Whether it's strip lights behind your TV, color-changing bulbs that let you set the mood, or backlit mirrors that make your space feel like a chill lounge, smart lighting just gets it right—no guesswork required.

I'm especially obsessed with my pink smart strip lights behind the TV. When I turn them on at night, it's like stepping into a glowy little cocoon. It literally transforms my space, easing me from day to night, from work mode to relaxation mode. Movie nights, and even just hanging out at home, feel like a special event.

Disco Ball Magic

In my opinion, disco balls are the MVP when it comes to making a statement with light. While not a direct light source, they are the drama queens of decor—always stealing the spotlight, but worth every glint. Disco balls remind me of the sparkling, festive energy of Indian fashion—especially the sequined partywear I grew up with: sparkly, joyful, and always a little extra. Whether it's an expensive piece from Rotganzen or an Amazon find, when the light hits just right, a disco ball scatters little sparks of lighting magic across the room. It's like sequins for your walls—the movement of those light spots makes the room come alive.

I first discovered the power of disco balls in an old apartment that barely got any direct light. Using fishing wire, I hung several disco balls of different sizes in the one spot that got an hour of sun. For that brief window of time when the sun hit them, my walls came alive with tiny, shimmering spots. It felt like I'd stumbled onto a secret. And it never got old—I was in awe every single time.

In my last place, I took it up a notch by DIY-ing pendant lights covered in disco mirrors. They hung over my kitchen island, catching the golden hour light and reflecting it in all directions. Every time this happened, I felt like a little kid who just learned a magic trick.

Command hooks and a little clear fishing wire are all it takes to bring serious disco-ball glamour to a corner that needs some sparkle.

Mixing Textures Adds Depth

Having multiple textures in one space is a way of shaking things up, even when everything else stays perfectly still. Textures are the fashion statements of your home—layered, unexpected, and full of personality. I first realized the power of texture when I paired black leather trousers with a black knit sweater. Same color, totally different vibe—smooth and shiny with soft and nubby. It just worked, and it taught me that mixing textures can add way more interest than just playing with color.

Texture adds depth and makes decor feel more lifelike. One of the coolest trends right now is 3D art, specifically pieces that look like food. Think candles shaped like avocados or a lamp that looks like a croissant. Artists really know how to use texture and contour to trick your eye and make everyday objects feel whimsical and unexpected.

One of my favorite examples is Ukrainian artist Julia Stankevych's 3D painting called *Bagel with Cream Cheese*. She uses modeling paste to create an actual cream cheese texture on the painted bagel, and when she shares her process online—applying the paste with a butter knife—it looks just like spreading cream cheese on a real bagel. That painting is on my wish list.

Another standout is Japanese designer Yukiko Morita's bread lamp, made from actual fermented bread. I used to own one—a croissant lamp with the same flaky texture as the real thing. Every time I turned it on, I had to remind myself not to take a bite. That's the kind of playful, lifelike touch that makes a space feel unique.

And texture goes beyond fabrics, finishes, and art—it can show up on walls too. I've seen people use moldings, shiplap, and beadboard to add dimension to plain walls. It's a great way to make a room feel richer without adding a bunch of stuff.

It's all about that push and pull—pairing leather with velvet, or mixing industrial stainless steel with warm wood. It's not just about variety; it's about creating a tactile experience that draws you in. One of my favorite combos I've used was the textured peel-and-stick tiles on my former kitchen island paired with soft velvet barstools. It was the balance between rough and smooth that made it feel thoughtfully put together, rather than just a random mix of materials.

When I paired a sleek marble coffee table with cozy bouclé ottomans, it felt like mixing silk with chunky knits—opposites that just click. The contrast made the whole space feel more dynamic.

One color, many textures. Pink rattan and velvet create a lush, richly layered feel in Averie's living room.

UNIVERSE

Creating Movement with Patterns

When it comes to playing with movement, it doesn't get more fun than patterns, whose lively colors and hypnotic motifs guide your eye through space. Patterns are also a great way to bring culture and individuality into your home. Every culture or country has its own traditional patterns that make an interior style easy to recognize. In India, there's no more recognizable pattern than traditional block prints. I've had the chance to visit block printing facilities in both Mumbai and Jaipur, and I even got to try my hand at the technique myself during fashion school. The final pattern is always beautiful, but what really stuck with me was the process—carving a wood block to create an intricate pattern, selecting colors, and dipping the block in dye before pressing it onto fabric. It's time-consuming, meticulous, and completely rewarding.

In one of my previous apartments, I painted a checkered wall that became a viral hit. The process was simple—taping and painting squares—but the final effect was bold, graphic, and oh-so-satisfying. I've been hooked on checks ever since. In fact, I love them so much that I've incorporated checks into every apartment that's followed. I once painted a plain white door in multicolored checks using leftover paints—it turned a boring door into a piece of art.

It's also fun to experiment with modern takes on patterns. Right now, fruit patterns are super popular in wallpapers, while pretty botanical prints stenciled onto walls can also add a beautiful, organic feel.

I love the idea of murals—big flowers or bold stripes that add personality to a space. I wish I had the confidence to freehand paint on walls, but for those like me who aren't quite there yet, stencils are an amazing option to get that artistic touch without the stress.

Textiles are another great way to bring patterns into your home without committing to paint. Think striped pillows, checkered rugs, printed throws, and bold bedding. Even upholstered pieces like chairs, ottomans, and lampshades can become pattern moments that add energy and vibrancy to your space. I've visited silk-weaving factories where they create elaborate sari patterns by weaving different types and colors of yarns together. Just watching that process is as inspiring as seeing the final product. I love how patterns can say so much about a place. The patterns you find in an old English castle are completely different from the ones in a Spanish palace, for example, yet both are deeply tied to their origins. Patterns are an awesome way to add your own story and individuality to your space.

How fun is this color-blocked door? It's an easy, renter-friendly way Lizzy added personality and punch to an often overlooked detail.

Mixing different patterns can feel risky, but when done right, it's like a visual dance. Combining stripes with checks or florals with abstract shapes can create a playful, layered aesthetic. One key tip: Scale matters. A small-scale print often pairs beautifully with a larger, bolder one, creating balance rather than competition. Even basic patterns like stripes and checks can be used in unexpected ways—like painting a bold, saturated, thick-striped pattern on an accent wall combined with adding small checks to a dresser. It's all about finding the right balance while keeping the vibe fun and unique.

Movement Matters—5 Key Takeaways

1. LIGHT BRINGS LIFE.
Layer natural and smart lighting to vibe-shift your space from morning motivation to evening chill.

2. DISCO BALLS ARE MAGIC.
Add reflective accents to amp up the energy and make your room feel like it's giving main character.

3. TEXTURE ADDS DEPTH.
Play with contrasts—like leather and velvet—to create tactile interest and visual appeal.

4. PATTERNS ARE PARAMOUNT.
Experiment with bold prints and unexpected combinations to guide the eye and add a dash of personality.

5. BALANCE IS KEY.
Mix lighting, texture, and patterns to keep your space feeling curated, not chaotic.

Designed by Ghislaine, this green plaid wallpaper sets the stage for a witty twist on a classic artwork. The pig side table is the perfect finishing touch.

Time for a Movement Checkup!

Ready to get your space moving? Take a second to answer these quick questions and find out if your room has the energy it needs to thrive.

1. What's your natural light situation?

- **A** Sunlight is my best friend, and it shows.
- **B** I have a few rays here and there, but not much to work with.
- **C** I'm pretty much in a cave.

2. How does your room feel when you walk in?

- **A** Like a burst of energy—vibrant, fresh, and full of life.
- **B** It's okay, but a bit flat sometimes.
- **C** It's mostly calm but feels . . . stagnant.

3. How do you use lighting to set the mood?

- **A** I layer it like a pro—ambient, task, and statement lighting all work together.
- **B** I've got a couple of lamps, but it could be more intentional.
- **C** I mostly rely on overhead lights (and they're a little too harsh).

4. What's the texture vibe in your space?

- **A** I mix leather, velvet, and soft fabrics—there's texture everywhere.
- **B** I have a few textures, but I could use more contrast.
- **C** Most of my textures are similar, with no real variation.

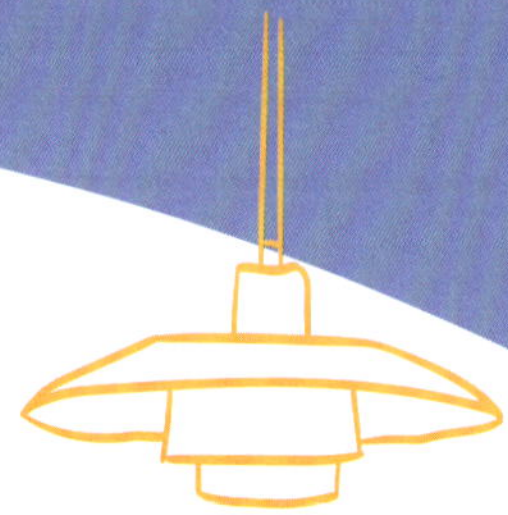

HOW DID YOU DO?

Mostly As

If you answered mostly As, you're already embracing movement like a pro! Your space is alive, layered, and full of personality.

Mostly Bs

If you answered mostly Bs, you're on the right track! A few tweaks with lighting, texture, and patterns will make your space feel more dynamic and engaging.

Mostly Cs

If you answered mostly Cs, it's time for a change! Add some texture, layers of lighting, and bold patterns to wake up your space and bring it to life.

HOME TOUR

Ghislaine Viñas

When Ghislaine Viñas designs a space—whether for a client or for herself—it's all about creating a sense of joy. It's what she calls the "Aesthetics of Happiness"—a philosophy perfectly aligned with the heart of dopamine decor.

Ghislaine's entryway is bursting with life thanks to sunny yellow doors and a combination of fresh and faux florals.

Born in the Netherlands, raised in South Africa, and now splitting her time between New York City and Tivoli in upstate New York, Ghislaine has carved out a globally celebrated career that spans residential, hospitality, product, and commercial design.

Known for her bold color choices, whimsical forms, and signature sense of humor, she brings a spirit of play and vibrancy to every project. Ghislaine's Tivoli home is proof that a space filled with color, memory, and intention doesn't just look great—it feels alive. Whether it's the playful pig table, a fluorescent red light, or artwork from her daughters, every detail carries a story. She doesn't play it safe—and that's exactly the point. Her home is a fearless reflection of what makes her happy, and a reminder that design is most powerful when it's personal. Forget the rules, skip the trends, and trust your gut. That's not just good design advice—it's good life advice.

How would you describe your design aesthetic?

My design philosophy revolves around the "Aesthetics of Happiness"—creating interiors that spark joy and comfort and have a sense of humor. For clients, it's always a collaborative process, discovering what happiness looks like for them and translating that into something beautiful and functional.

My own home in Tivoli was different—it was more of a curation process, built from pieces I had collected over time. It came together organically, resulting in a mix that feels spontaneous, eclectic, and less about trying to be surprising and more about embracing what was already there.

Which items in your home would be the most coveted in a future estate sale?

Definitely my John Wayne bust, which I found in Pennsylvania nearly twenty years ago. It's such an unexpected piece and always greets guests when they walk in.

I'd also say the David Chipperfield chairs in the kitchen—they were a gift from a client who was moving out of an apartment, and they're so beautifully designed. And then there's my Mark Mulroney piece, which brings this quirky, wacky energy I love. He's a longtime collaborator, and his work never fails to make me smile.

Oh, and the Tom Dixon fluorescent chairs in the dining room. I got them at a warehouse sale in SoHo years ago. The color just grabbed me. They're so simple, but that neon hue makes them a total statement.

White meets orange in this breezy bathroom. A duck-shaped vase and bold rug bring the fun.

Ghislaine's bedroom gets the balance right—warm neutrals plus surprise color and quirky details.

Classic meets quirky in Ghislaine's living room, thanks to a stunning mix of patterned wallpaper, traditional furniture, and unexpected art.

If your home had a theme song, what would it be and why?

The Pippi Longstocking theme song! I've always loved Pippi—she lives life like it's an adventure and finds fun in everything. Cleaning the kitchen becomes whimsical. That spirit of curiosity and joy is something I try to channel in my spaces. (Also, I love her hair.)

How does your home reflect your happiest memories?

It's filled with art, trinkets, and objects I've picked up on my travels, so there's a story behind everything. But what makes it most special is all the artwork from my daughters over the years. My home is colorful, layered, personal, and full of life—which is exactly how I want it to feel.

This bathroom's cafe curtain and strategic pops of color make the space shine.

Ghislaine at home.

What's your favorite hidden or unexpected detail in your home that guests might overlook?

Animals have made their way into nearly every room, without my even realizing it—through art, lighting, cabinetry, furniture. There's the swinging Seletti lamp in the kitchen and the Moooi pig table, to name just two things. They just keep appearing, and I've embraced it.

Also, many of the textiles and furnishings are my own designs, like the wallpaper I created for Wolf Gordon and the sofas and fireplace chairs from my HBF Textiles collab. Being surrounded by my own work makes it feel that much more personal.

Are there any design "rules" you love breaking?

The only rules I really follow are about proportion, because those are rooted in real design principles. But when it comes to aesthetics—mixing pieces, playing with color—there are no rules. Everyone has different things that bring them joy, and that's what should lead the way.

How does your home reflect your childhood influences or cultural background?

I'm Dutch, and I grew up in South Africa. My family didn't take things too seriously, and I think that shows in how I design. There's this mix of openness, adaptability, and a deep love for humor that shaped me. I like to go design off-roading, take risks, and do things that feel exciting and fun. Design should never be boring.

What's your secret to scoring the best vintage or secondhand finds?

Patience is everything. If something feels too curated, I'm not that into it. I love the treasure hunt—finding that one incredible piece in a place no one expects. I'll go to little towns, off-the-radar spots, anywhere that might hold a hidden gem. I'm drawn to pieces others might overlook.

Do you have a "no regrets" splurge item that instantly sparks joy?

Definitely adding windows to the kitchen and opening up the space to take in views of our property. It was a splurge during the renovation but totally worth it. Now when we're making coffee or cooking, my husband and I find ourselves just staring outside, naming the animals that wander by. It changed how we experience the home every day.

If your walls could talk, what would they say about your design journey?

They'd probably say, "Enough with the moving things around already!" I'm constantly rearranging—art, furniture, accessories. It keeps the space feeling fresh, alive, and creatively stimulating.

In the dining room: neon Tom Dixon chairs, superhero art, and shapely candles meet a classic wood table. It works—and wows.

This John Wayne head bust in Ghislaine's living room never fails to spark conversation.

What brands or designers do you keep coming back to when decorating your home?

Moooi—their Dutch sensibility and sense of humor are unmatched. I also love Patricia Urquiola, Paola Navone, and Nathalie Du Pasquier. Their designs bring that perfect mix of unexpected and bold that I find so inspiring.

How do you balance function with fun in your decor?

It starts with architecture and proportion—understanding how a room flows, how it's used. Once that's in place, I look for "activation points"—spots where I can add color, texture, or unexpected pieces that give the room energy and life. The balance between scale and surprise is what makes a space work.

What DIY project or personal touch in your home means the most to you?

The powder room! It's this tiny jewel box of a space, with two shades of green color-blocked on the walls and a fluorescent red light fixture. The gallery wall of portraits is my favorite part. There's work by Mark Mulroney and by my daughter Saskia, and I've even named all the women in the portraits. They've become part of the home's personality.

What are some of your happy colors or color combinations?

Green is the dominant color in this house—it just felt right, especially being surrounded by rolling hills. I love pairing it with fluorescent red for a jolt of energy.

I'm also into combos like mustard yellow and pink, or powder blue and bright red. There are no bad color combinations—it's all about how you use and balance them. A country home doesn't need to follow the usual subdued palette. It should reflect the energy and spirit of the people living in it.

Any advice for someone wanting to incorporate dopamine decor into their space?

Dopamine decor doesn't mean chaos. It can be bold and joyful while still feeling curated and personal.

Start by figuring out what makes you happy—what makes you smile. Take photos of things you're drawn to, write down what resonates. From there, start building a personal visual language—something that feels like your own internal design compass.

Ghislaine's DOPAMENU

• APPETIZERS •

Add a pop of neon to your space for a change in energy.

Play with animal-inspired decor, from lamps to cabinetry, to layer in unexpected elements.

• MAINS •

Curate a mix of items over time to create an eclectic space.

Reimagine your rooms by switching up layouts and furniture placements.

• DESSERT •

Create arrangements with fresh flowers and produce from your own garden.

CHAPTER FIVE

MOTIVATION

Finding Your Drive Through Design

Lockers are one of my favorite small space storage solutions. This lilac-painted locker doubles as storage and a style statement.

Motivation is one of those things that can be annoyingly elusive—like your phone charger when you're running on 2 percent battery. One minute you're ready to conquer the world (or at least your messy desk), and the next, you're watching Instagram Reels on productivity hacks instead of actually . . . you know . . . being productive (no judgment; we've all done it).

But what if your space and decor could actually give you a little motivational nudge, and with that, a boost of dopamine? Spoiler: It totally can.

The Power of Space to Motivate

Space in my childhood apartment in Mumbai was tight, which made organization a constant challenge and inspiration hard to come by. My mom did her best with two young kids, but it's tough to make a cramped space feel like a sanctuary when four people share it. I remember thinking, *One day, I'm going to have my own place, and it's going to be organized, calming, and full of good vibes.*

That idea stuck with me and followed me throughout adulthood. Even as I moved through different small apartments over the years, I made sure each space was organized to feel inspiring, no matter the square footage. Whether it's a cozy studio or a one-bedroom filled with sunlight (shout-out to my current place), creating a motivating space has always been my goal.

Why Motivation Needs Organization

It sounds a little unglamorous, but honestly, clutter is the ultimate motivation and vibe killer. It's like trying to do yoga on a floor covered in laundry—impossible. There's nothing inspiring about tripping over yesterday's jeans while trying to get your morning routine going. That's why, to me, organizing a space is even more important than decorating it. You can't really vibe with a room that's chaos incarnate.

For me, everything has its place—like Ari's wardrobe of tiny outfits neatly organized in a colorful locker that doubles as decor. It's not just cute; it's efficient. The more you cut down on mess, the easier it is to move through your space without tripping over stuff (literally and mentally). The goal is to create a space that works with you, not against you.

Sometimes, organizing can even feel therapeutic. Imagine putting on your favorite playlist, slipping on your headphones, and diving into a cleaning or organizing session. The rhythm of tidying up your space can be almost as fulfilling as a therapy session—a little reset for both your surroundings and your mind.

Setting Yourself Up for Success

Your space can set the tone for how motivated you feel. One of my biggest lessons in this came from my time in fashion school. I was juggling classes like patternmaking and personal grooming (yes, makeup class was a thing), and I learned quickly that staying organized was the only way to stay sane. I had different kits and boxes for sewing tools, art supplies, and cosmetics—all labeled and easy to grab. That way, I wasn't scrambling for a specific thread or a pair of scissors every time I needed them.

My last apartment taught me the same lesson in a different way. I never enjoyed cooking much, but my bright, airy kitchen—and a growing addiction to Seamless—made me want to change that.

I organized the space to make cooking feel easier, prettier, and more accessible. Who knew adding wallpaper inside cabinets, using cute shelf risers, and neatly labeling my spice jars were all it would take to unleash my inner chef? Now I cook and eat at home more than ever, and I love it. It's amazing how a dash of order and a pinch of style can instantly take a task from daunting to enjoyable.

And here's an unexpected bonus to setting up your space for success: The act of organizing can actually be a creative outlet in and of itself. I've found that cleaning or rearranging my space sometimes gives me new ideas—like the time I organized my desk and made a video about it. The clean, colorful layout with my quirky organizers (like the mini NYC trash can for pens) became a hit with my followers. And because my desk continues to inspire me every day, it's the gift that keeps on giving.

LEFT When closets go open-concept, fashion (and function) become the decor. Even Ari gets a wardrobe moment.
PAGES 188–189 In my first studio, color popped in every corner—from the pink radiator to books styled in the fireplace.

will Always
be New York
or Nowhere
FLOWER MARKET
TOKYO

WE DON'T
HAVE TO BE
ORDINARY

Routine Is Your Bestie

Another lesson I've learned from organizing my spaces? Clean as you go. This philosophy keeps me grounded, even when life feels overwhelming. I shoot a lot of brand content in my apartment, which leads to inevitable clutter. But even if it's late at night, I can't go to bed without putting everything back.

And it doesn't stop there. The second I come in from a walk with Ari, I grab the cleaning kit I keep by the door and wipe his paws. My jacket, Ari's winter clothes, and even my hair ties go straight into their designated spots the second they come off. Whether it's putting away groceries as soon as I come back from the store or cleaning up while waiting for my pasta to boil, I always make it a point to tackle little tasks as they come up.

It's that sense of resetting the space that keeps me calm and motivated. It's not about being obsessive—it's about knowing that an organized space makes the next day feel lighter and more productive.

This is why I'm not a fan of leaving things for a "deep clean" day because let's be honest—saving everything for one big cleaning day feels a little like throwing your future self under the bus. Not cool.

LEFT Averie proves that even kitchen storage can be delightful. Hot pink cubes? Yes, please.
RIGHT Michael's colorful crates add both form and function—stylish storage with a healthy hit of dopamine.

But while the clean-as-you-go approach works for me, you might be more of a Sunday-reset kind of person, and that's totally okay too. The key is finding what fits your life and keeps your space—and mind—feeling calm.

Make Motivation Look Cute

Motivation doesn't have to feel like a chore. It can be as simple as setting up a mini coffee station that makes your mornings feel a little more luxurious or having a decorative box to keep all your remote controls in check. You know, the ones that multiply like rabbits when you're not looking—like, I'm pretty sure I bought only one remote, not a small village of them.

A few years ago, the organizing options were pretty standard—think basic plastic cubes and containers. They did the job but didn't really bring any joy. But these days? You don't have to choose between function and beauty. Brands have caught on to the idea that storage can offer both. Whether you prefer minimal and chic or colorful and quirky, there's something out there for everyone. Lately, I've been really into super fun boxes that look like coffee table books—perfect for storing essential but unaesthetic stuff. Little things like that not only reduce visual clutter but also make daily tasks feel more intentional and satisfying.

There's no doubt that organizing can 100 percent double as dopamine decor. For instance, I have a cute pear-shaped organizer from MoMA Design Store that went viral on my social media. It holds pens and clips but looks like an oversized piece of fruit—a total serotonin boost for my desk.

When it comes to organizing products that combine function with flair, my go-to brands are Yamazaki, Open Spaces, and the Container Store. They put as much thought into design as they do into functionality. I also love finding quirky, stylish options at places like MoMA Design Store, Hay, and IKEA. Whether it's a chic shelf riser or a colorful storage box, the right products make staying organized way more fun.

My last two apartments had tiny kitchens, so I got creative with storage. I found a tall industrial-style shelf from Hay, styled it with colorful appliances, and even added a fruit-print peel-and-stick wallpaper to make it pop. In my last place, with so many windows and few walls, I invested in the Story Bookcase from Design Within Reach. It's perfect for small corners and makes the most of the height without taking up precious floor space.

If you're looking for a low-cost and renter-friendly hack, I'm obsessed with IKEA's paper storage boxes. They're foldable, portable, and perfect for keeping things organized without breaking the bank. For renters who want to avoid drilling holes, clear acrylic stick-on shelves are a game-changer, especially in the bathroom.

When you make your space feel both functional *and* fun, surrounding yourself with things that make you happy, motivation is sure to follow.

A Clutter-Free Mindset

An organized space leads to an organized mind. For me, moving is a prime opportunity for decluttering—mentally and physically. Moving is my opportunity to reset and make sure I'm not holding on to things that weigh me down.

But even if you're not starting over in a new place, you can still do an occasional audit of your home to make sure everything you have still feels functional and useful. Twice a year, I like to take stock of what I actually use, and if I haven't touched it in the last six months, it gets donated, recycled, or listed on Facebook Marketplace. (Honestly, if it hasn't been used in half a year, it's probably just living rent-free in my space.)

So how do you decide what to keep and what to toss? I'm a big fan of Marie Kondo's "spark joy" rule. I buy things I love, but I also get sent a lot of PR packages. Storage boxes fill up fast, and clutter can sneak in before you know it. So, only a few cherished items make the cut when it comes to holding on to things purely for memory's sake.

I also declutter after a big DIY or art project when I need to reorganize supplies. And I donate clothes and decor regularly to my neighborhood charity—being mindful about what I keep and buy helps me do my part for sustainable living and reduces waste.

Plus, the more I let go of unnecessary stuff, the more room I have for things that actually spark joy. Since I work with brands and often get new decor, I have to stay on top of things to avoid feeling overwhelmed. Every once in a while I do think about a piece I've given away and wish I had it back, but then I remind myself that nostalgia isn't a good enough reason to live in a clutter museum.

I'd rather live in a space that feels calm and intentional than hold on to things just in case. It's a lesson I had to learn after moving apartments so many times—keeping only what you really love makes your home feel lighter and more curated. And there's nothing more motivating than that.

This desk setup is the ideal mix of work and play: smart storage, fun colors, and shelves with serious personality.

LONDON
WHO'S AFRAID OF PINK, ORANGE & GREEN?
Vivid

NIKE
NIKE

Motivation Moves—5 Key Takeaways

1. START SMALL.
Tackle one space at a time. For instance, organize your desk before diving into your whole room.

2. GET INTO A ROUTINE.
Don't save cleaning for a marathon session. Cleaning and tidying a little bit every day keeps your space manageable.

3. MAKE IT FUN.
Use cute organizers, colorful storage containers, or quirky decor items to make tidying up feel less like a task.

4. SET UP ZONES.
Create dedicated areas for work, relaxation, and creativity. This helps keep your mind on task and your space functional.

5. CLEAR AS YOU GO.
Whether it's a photoshoot mess or the dinner dishes, put things back in their place as soon as you're done. Future You will be grateful.

Marianne Plaisance's closet is anything but ordinary—cow print, cherries, and chic organization come together beautifully.

Organizer Matchup
Guess the Use

Let's make organizing a little more fun! Below are photos of a few quirky organizers. Can you guess what each one is meant to hold? Match each organizer to its perfect use from the list below—then check your answers at the end!

OPTIONS TO MATCH:

A Coats, bags, and hats
B Desk essentials such as pens, paperclips, and sticky notes
C Tools, art supplies, or craft materials
D Mugs, glasses, or small kitchen items
E Shower toiletries and skincare

NOW, MATCH EACH PHOTO TO ITS LETTER:

1

2

3

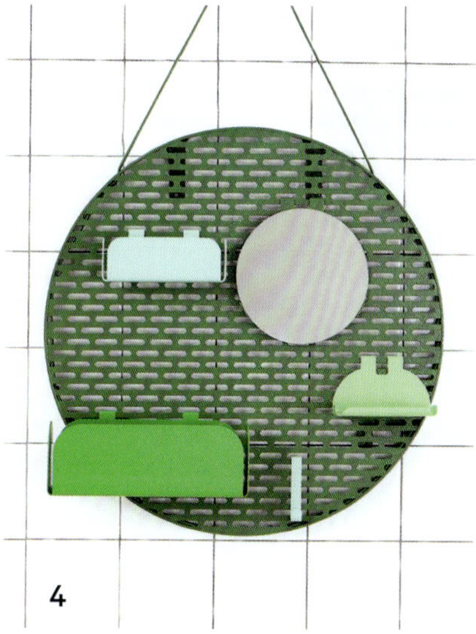

4

5

Answer Key

1. *C—Tools, art supplies, or craft materials*
   Toyo ST-350 Tool Box—MoMA Design Store
2. *B—Desk essentials such as pens, paperclips, and sticky notes.* Pear Pod Multifunctional Desktop Organizer—MoMA Design Store
3. *A—Coats, bags, and hats*
   Heller Swell Wall Hook—Hellerware
4. *E—Shower toiletries and skincare*
   The Spot Sky Modular Shower Organizer—Quiet Town
5. *D—Mugs, glasses, or small kitchen items*
   Kalager Design Cup Rack—Kalager Design

HOME TOUR

Maitri Mody

Welcome to my last Brooklyn apartment—where the pages of this book came to life. As the author of *Dopamine Design,* I wanted to share a more detailed glimpse into one of my own spaces, which became a living experiment in the power of joyful design. This apartment became so much more than a place to live; it's where I created, tested ideas, and found comfort. It's a reflection of my personality: colorful, playful, and ever-evolving. I hope it inspires you to embrace your own style with fearless creativity.

Oven Control
Front
Rear
Rear
Front
Power Boil

Whether it's a wraparound balcony in Brooklyn or a single patch of wall painted in your favorite color, your space has the power to reflect not just who you are but also who you're becoming. There's no final form when it comes to joyful design. Just a series of choices, instincts, and experiments that add up to something unmistakably you. So go ahead: Swap the pillows, paint the ceiling, hang that weird art. Your home is your canvas. Keep making it yours.

How would you describe your design aesthetic?

Colorful, playful, whimsical, and always evolving. I love a lot of different design styles and aesthetics, related to both fashion and interiors. I prefer to mix different design aesthetics rather than commit to one.

Which items in your home would be the most coveted in a future estate sale?

My vintage Serpentine lamp, designed by Jack Haywood for Modeline in the 1970s. And my Lenox Spice Village 2024 reissue—which will probably be considered vintage in the future.

If your home had a theme song, what would it be and why?

"Happy" by Pharrell Williams. It's like instant therapy for me when I feel low. My home makes me feel exactly the same way—it's also my therapist .

How does your home reflect your happiest memories?

Once a year, for Diwali, my brother and I got to shop for new clothes. It was the happiest time of the year for me. I would pick out the most colorful and garish clothes and then style my outfits in unexpected and weird ways. My parents gave me full creative freedom.

And now I get to do the same with my home! I get to dress it up in whatever I want and express myself creatively through my space.

PAGE 199 In my last Brooklyn apartment, a petite dining nook with hidden storage was my favorite place for taking in sunsets and skyline. **LEFT** Don't overlook the stove! Shelves over the range offer extra storage and a chance to showcase cheerful decor.

An Ari-inspired coffee table and a wall of dopamine decor tie this living room to the dreamy bedroom beyond.

JUL
20
SUN
HOW TO LIVE WITH OBJECTS
THE NEW BOHEMIANS
ICONIC ROOMS

What's your favorite hidden or unexpected detail in your home that guests might overlook?

I'd say the patio—having a wraparound balcony is a rare gem in NYC, where outdoor space is hard to come by. It wrapped around the apartment and offered some pretty stunning skyline views. At night, when the lights came on, it felt especially magical.

Are there any design "rules" you love breaking?

I've never had any formal training in interior design—my background is in fashion—so I tend to approach decorating the same way I approach styling an outfit: instinct first, rules second (or not at all). I like learning about design principles, but when it comes time to actually create a space, I rarely think about them. So I guess I'm breaking all the rules . . . maybe even without realizing it.

How does your home reflect your childhood influences or cultural background?

As a child, I used to dream about having my own space one day, even if it was just a room. I spent countless hours imagining—and sometimes even sketching—how it would look.

And now that I live on my own (with my furry roommate, of course), I'm fulfilling all my childhood dreams—truly owning my space and making it my own. The joy of finally having my own apartment is reflected in its playful, vibrant energy. It's a mix of high and low pieces, which has been the perfect way to make the space feel elevated without overspending.

What's your secret to scoring the best vintage or secondhand finds?

I make regular stops at my local vintage stores—usually while I'm out walking my dog. Even if I come up empty a few times, there's always a chance I'll get lucky next time. I also love checking out vintage shops when I travel and usually do a little research beforehand to scout out the best spots. Stooping in NYC led to some amazing (and surprisingly high-quality) finds, and of course, I'm always browsing Facebook Marketplace and eBay—some of my favorite pieces have come from there.

Do you have a "no regrets" splurge item that instantly sparks joy?

My custom pug coffee table, without a doubt. I waited nearly a year to buy it after getting the initial quote—it felt like such a splurge. But I couldn't shake the idea, so I finally went for it. And honestly? Zero regrets. Every time I see Ari next to the table, it makes me smile. Even on the gloomiest days, it brings me joy.

Ari and I in our very first studio apartment—where the joy began.

If your walls could talk, what would they say about your design journey?

They'd probably say, "So . . . when are we getting painted back to white?" or maybe, "Don't worry—I won't tell the landlord." I've moved almost every couple of years for the past six years, and each time, I've added color and personality—then repainted everything back to white before moving out. Even in rentals, I've always refused to live with boring white walls. Life's too short not to love your space. Now that I finally own my home in Portland, Maine, my walls no longer have to worry about being painted back to white. But, they'll be happy to know I'm planning on adding more color or layering on a new shade.

Sometimes the smallest accents have the biggest impact. Even bookends can be decor when they're this cute.

Green peel-and-stick tiles, chili pepper knobs, and a surprise pop on the pillar make this rental kitchen totally me.

What brands or designers do you keep coming back to when decorating your home?

Design Within Reach, Society 6, Etsy, MoMA Design Store, Rebel Walls for wallpaper, HomeGoods, and many more.

How do you balance function with fun in your decor?

I've always lived in small apartments, so making the most of my space is second nature. That mindset shows up in my decor too—I gravitate toward pieces that are both functional and fun. Think storage furniture that doubles as a design moment, or playful hooks that work hard and look good doing it.

Which DIY project or personal touch in your home means the most to you?

One of my favorite DIYs was the pendant lamps over my kitchen island. I added disco mirrors to some Verner Panton Flowerpot lamp dupes. During the golden hour and at sunset, the light would hit them just right—the walls and ceiling would sparkle. Even after seeing it countless times, it brought me the same joy every single time.

What are some of your happy colors or color combinations?

There are way too many to name—but pink and red is my ultimate happy combo. I love mixing contrasting colors, but there's something especially satisfying about pairing neighbors on the color wheel. Pink and orange, blue and green . . . those combos just click. And honestly? Anything with lilac. Lilac and yellow, lilac and green, lilac and orange, lilac and red—I'm clearly in a long-term relationship with lilac.

Any advice for someone wanting to incorporate dopamine decor into their space?

Don't overthink design rules, chase trends, or feel like you have to stick to one aesthetic. Start small—add colors or pieces that genuinely make you happy. Love Danish pastels *and* bohemian vibes? Mix them! The magic happens when you blend what you love into something that feels like *you*. Create your own aesthetic—and hey, give it a name while you're at it.

If there's one thing I've learned, it's that home isn't about getting everything "right." It's about making space for the things that bring you joy—no matter how quirky, colorful, or unexpected they might be. My apartment is a happy blend of memories, creativity, and experimentation. And yours can be too.

The sweetest Ari tribute—custom-made and pug-approved.

Maitri's DOPAMENU

• APPETIZERS •

Swap out basic switches and outlet covers for ones with fun shapes, colors, or patterns.

DIY a disco mirror light fixture, or add a touch of the unexpected to functional items.

• MAINS •

Paint an accent wall in a checkerboard or color-block pattern.

Add peel-and-stick wallpaper in a bold pattern.

• DESSERT •

Make your kitchen a mood with playful ceramics and colorful dishware.

The Brooklyn skyline sets the scene on this cozy balcony. Pineapple rug, lemon stool, and a toucan pillow keep it lighthearted.

A berry print shower curtain and sleek over-the-shower organizer deliver delight and smart utility to this tiny bathroom.

Acknowledgments

Thank you to my beloved pug and best friend, Ari—my constant source of joy, my biggest dopamine boost, and the unexpected beginning of it all.

To my mom, for enrolling me in everything from karate to dance to charcoal painting as a kid. You opened up my world to new ideas and believed in every quirky outfit I wore and every unconventional idea I shared.

To my parents, for giving me the freedom to find my own path.

To Cristina, for not only being an incredible editor but also a true creative partner and friend. From matching wallpapers to choosing the same rug, this collaboration felt like a little bit of fate. Thank you for guiding me with such care while still giving me the freedom to play.

To Amanda, my literary agent, for being the first to truly see the vision for this book and helping build the foundation it stands on. Thank you for answering every random question and guiding me through this process with patience and clarity.

Thank you to Kamala for helping shape my ideas into words and keeping me organized from day one. I'm grateful for your talent, wit, and dedication throughout this journey.

To Isabelle Giofreddi, for designing this book and bringing the vision in my head to life. Thank you for infusing it with the playfulness and joy I had always imagined.

To Averie, Ghislaine, Marianne, Michelle and Forrest, Michael, Jassy, and Lizzy—thank you for welcoming us into your beautiful, creative, and joyful homes, and for being part of my very first book.

And to anyone who finds themselves starting life over again: Healing may feel far away, but it isn't. Sometimes it begins with small, intentional choices—choosing joy, surrounding yourself with what lights you up, and allowing yourself to build a life that feels like home.

Resources

Paint Colors That Shaped My Homes

PAGE 8: wall, Comical Coral by Sherwin Williams; dresser, Pink Azalea by Benjamin Moore; door, Green 13 by Lick

PAGE 10: wall, Pop by Clare Paint; dresser, Joyful Lilac by YesColours

PAGE 19: Joyful Lilac by YesColours

PAGE 32: pink accent wall, Joyful Pink and Calming Green by YesColours; arch, Joyful Lilac and Friendly Pink by YesColours

PAGE 65: Flower Girl by Behr

PAGE 107: Italiano Rose, Hydrangea, Parrot Green, Pink Begonia, Glen Ridge Gold, and Anderson Blue by Benjamin Moore

PAGE 111: Nancy's Blushes by Farrow & Ball

PAGE 114: painted mirror, Dark Salmon and Valentine's Day by Benjamin Moore

PAGE 156–157: Pop by Clare Paint

PAGE 188: Green 13 by Lick

PAGE 193, CLOCKWISE FROM LEFT: Pop and Lemonade by Clare Paint, Joyful Lilac, Calming Green, and Friendly Pink by YesColours

PAGE 199: Nairobi Blue by Clare Paint

PAGE 205: Little Dipper by Benjamin Moore in cabinet and trim finish

Brands I Own (and Obsess Over)

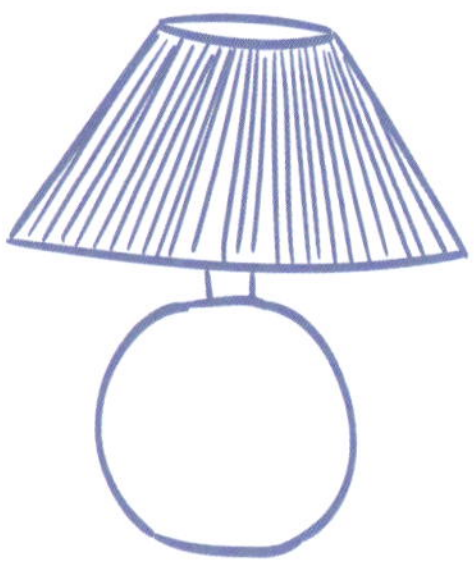

Wallpaper

Chasing Paper
Otto Studio
Rebel Walls
Society 6
Spoonflower
Wall Pops

Lighting

CB2
Herman Miller
Louis Poulsen
Luminaire Authentik
Pooky Lighting
Stray Dog Designs
Studio Limonada
Verner Panton

Hardware

Etsy
Fantini Rubinetti
Ferguson Home
Hapny Home
Matilda Goad
Perigold
Plank Hardware

Rugs

Angela Adams
Cold Picnic
Layered
Nordic Knots
Pieces Home
Revival
Society 6
Tarta Gelatina

Art

Affordable Art Fair
Animalist
FY!
Lumas
Peleton
Saatchi Art
Sally Muir
Society 6

Playful Home Decor

Anthropologie
Ban.do
Damson Madder
Gustaf Westman
Helle Mardahl
HomeGoods
H&M Home
Lenox
Maison Balzac
Marimekko
MoMA Design Store
Urban Outfitters
Zara Home

Chic Storage Solutions

Hay Design
IKEA
Mustard Made
Open Spaces
Yamazaki Home

Furniture

All Modern
Design Within Reach
Dowel Jones
Heller
Hem
Kartell
Lulu & Georgia
Montana Furniture
Muuto
OMHU CPH
Room & Board
Sun at Six
Sundays
Thuma
Tylko
USM Modular Furniture
Vitra

Vintage Stores

1stDibs
Amsterdam Modern
Betsu Studio
Chairish
Kooloo Modern
Merit
Mid Century Friends
Renew Finds
Sunbeam Vintage
The Millie Vintage

Ceramics Worth Collecting

Atelier Beroj
Hal Haines
Hannah Simpson Studio
Laetitia Rouget
Mud Witch
Salkeramik
Swedenland Ceramics
Toni Darling Frank
Wobbly Studio

About the Author

Maitri Mody is an interior decorator and founder of @honeyidressedthepug. With a background shaped by living and working across Mumbai, New York City, and London, she brings a global, fashion-informed perspective to home design. Drawing from her experience as an editorial and costume stylist, she creates colorful, functional spaces that prioritize joy, individuality, and emotional connection. Her work has been featured in *The New York Times*, Apartment Therapy, *Better Homes & Gardens*, and more.

Me and my best boy Ari—at home in every sense of the word.

Photographer Credits

Sylvie Li
Pages 1, 15, 37, 38, 40–41, 42–43, 44, 45, 46–47, 48, and 194.

Boz Gagovski
Pages 12–13, 72, 79, 80, 82–83, 84–85, 86, 87, 88–89, 90, 119, and 191.

Erin Austen Abbott
Pages 23, 35, 51, 52, 54–55, 56–57, 58, 59, 60–61, 62, and 224.

Erin Derby
Pages 2, 6–7, 21, 24, 29, 30, 68, 70, 71, 93, 94, 96–97, 98–99, 100, 101, 102–103, 104, 107, 110, 111, 113, 114, 115, 116, 120, 121, 125, 126, 128–129, 130, 131, 132–133, 134, 161, 162, 165, 169, 171, 172–173, 174–175, 176, 177, 178–179, 180, 190, 199, 200, 202–203, 205, 206–207, 208, 210–211, 212, 217, and 222–223.

Tropico Photo
Pages 73, 137, 138, 140–141, 142–143, 144, 145, 146–147, and 148.

Erin Derby for Apartment Therapy
Pages 8, 10, 11, 16, 19, 27, 32, 65, 74, 156–157, 158, 183, 186, 188–189, 193, 204, and 221.

RIGHT Who says radiators can't be cute? A coat of pink paint gave this one an upgrade. **PAGES 222–223** Tiny but mighty, this living room brings together color, charm, and a whole lot of character.

DABITO
OLD BRAND NEW

Better
20
SUN

TEN SPEED PRESS
An imprint of the Crown Publishing Group
A division of Penguin Random House LLC
1745 Broadway
New York, NY 10019
tenspeed.com
penguinrandomhouse.com

Typefaces: Klim Type Foundry's Calibre, Emyself Design's ED Nimpkish, and Colophon Foundry's Raisonne

Library of Congress Cataloging-in-Publication Data
Names: Mody, Maitri author Title: Dopamine design: creating a home that makes you happy / Maitri Mody. Identifiers: LCCN 2025044270 (print) | LCCN 2025044271 (ebook) | ISBN 9780593838167 hardcover | ISBN 9780593838174 ebook Subjects: LCSH: Interior decoration—Themes, motives | Interior decoration | LCGFT: Illustrated works | Illustrated works Classification: LCC NK2110 .M635 2026 (print) | LCC NK2110 (ebook)

LC record available at https://lccn.loc.gov/2025044270

LC ebook record available at https://lccn.loc.gov/2025044271

Hardcover ISBN 978-0-593-83816-7
Ebook ISBN 978-0-593-83817-4

Editors: Cristina Garces and Dena Rayess | Production editor: Ashley Pierce
Designer: Isabelle Gioffredi | Production designer: Mari Gill
Production: Kim Tyner
Managing Editor: Kristin Sargianis | Copy editor: Sibylle Kazeroid
Proofreaders: Rachel Holzman and Sasha Tropp | Compositor: Hannah Hunt
Publicist: Natalie Yera-Campbell | Marketer: Andrea Portanova

Manufactured in China

10 9 8 7 6 5 4 3 2 1

First Edition

The authorized representative in the EU for product safety and compliance is Penguin Random House Ireland, Morrison Chambers, 32 Nassau Street, Dublin D02 YH68, Ireland, https://eu-contact.penguin.ie.